The Wesleyan Way

The Wesleyan Way

Book
Presents the beliefs and practices of Wesleyan Christianity in eight chapters, through story and Scripture, for individual or group use.
978-1-4267-6756-2

DVD
Features inspiring and moving interviews with eight Christian leaders who tell their faith stories. Interviews are about ten minutes long.
978-1-4267-6758-6

Leader Guide
Gives leaders everything they need to organize and run a group to study *The Wesleyan Way* in eight sessions. Includes pre-class planning, scheduling options, activities, and discussion questions for Scripture, book, and DVD.
978-1-4267-6757-9

For more information, go to www.TheWesleyanWay.com.

The Wesleyan Way

A Faith That Matters

SCOTT J. JONES

Abingdon Press
Nashville

The Wesleyan Way
A Faith That Matters

This book is printed on acid-free, elemental chlorine-free paper.

Library of Congress Cataloging-in-Publication applied for.

ISBN 978-1-4267-6756-2

Unless otherwise noted, all quotations from *The Works of John Wesley* are taken from the Bicentennial Edition of *The Works of John Wesley*, ed. W. Reginald Ward and Richard P. Heitzenrater (Nashville: Abingdon Press, 2005).

All quotations marked UMH are taken from *The United Methodist Hymnal*, copyright © 1989 by The United Methodist Publishing House. Used by permission.

All quotations marked BOD are from *The Book of Discipline of the United Methodist Church*, 2012. Copyright © 2013 by The United Methodist Publishing House. Used by permission.

Scripture quotations unless noted otherwise are from the Common English Bible. Copyright © 2011 by the Common English Bible. All rights reserved. Used by permission. www.CommonEnglishBible.com.

Scripture quotations marked NRSV are from the New Revised Standard Version of the Bible, copyright 1989, Division of Christian Education of the National Council of the Churches of Christ in the United States of America. Used by permission. All rights reserved.

Scripture quotations marked KJV are from The Authorized (King James) Version. Rights in the Authorized Version in the United Kingdom are vested in the Crown. Reproduced by permission of the Crown's patentee, Cambridge University Press.

Scripture quotations marked NIV are taken from the Holy Bible, New International Version®, NIV®. Copyright © 1973, 1978, 1984, 2011 by Biblica, Inc.™ Used by permission of Zondervan. All rights reserved worldwide. www.zondervan.com. The "NIV" and "New International Version" are trademarks registered in the United States Patent and Trademark Office by Biblica, Inc.™

14 15 16 17 18 19 20—10 9 8 7 6 5 4 3

MANUFACTURED IN THE UNITED STATES OF AMERICA

To L. Gregory Jones,
my brother, friend, colleague,
and inspiration along the way

Contents

Invitation

You are invited!

You are invited to walk the way of salvation, to live a life that matters, to connect with God's purposes for you and the world. It is a lifelong journey, and we take it one step at a time.

Yet, there are people who want to see a road map for the whole journey. These are the ones who ask, "Where are we going?" and "How long will it take?" They often ask, "How will we get there?" and "Do we have what it takes to make the trip?"

If you're one of those people, this program is for you. Or, if you find yourself mentoring or talking with one of those people, this program is for you. In both cases, you want and need to go deeper into understanding what the Christian life is all about.

I had that experience in the spring of 1978. I had finally resolved my spiritual search and had become a Christian. I had even started seminary, because I sensed that the church was a good thing and I wanted to help people find God. But I didn't know where it was all going or how it would work out.

My first-semester classes were more challenging and confusing than helpful. But then I enrolled in a course called "Wesley and the Wesleyan Tradition," taught by Dr. Albert Outler. Through a series of lectures, assigned readings, and one-on-one conversations, Dr. Outler helped me understand the way of salvation taught by the Bible, as understood by John Wesley and his brother Charles, evangelical reformers who lived and taught in the eighteenth century. In the process, I was shocked and surprised to learn that Wesley's understanding of Christianity was the official teaching of my own church! I was the son, grandson, and great-grandson of United Methodist pastors, and somehow I had never learned the Wesleyan Way of salvation.

I don't want that to happen to you. I want you to see what God has in store for you, so you'll have a more complete picture of the Christian life and how it might work for you, your family, your friends, and everyone else with whom you come into contact.

When I first started learning the Wesleyan Way, it gave me a framework to resolve some of the biggest and most important questions of my life. When I hear criticisms of Christianity, I often think, *They are not talking about the Wesleyan Way.* When I read about people's struggles with deep questions of faith, I think, *If only I could share the Wesleyan Way with them.*

That's why I'm writing this study. It's why I've invited some of today's most exciting and compelling Christian leaders to share their thoughts and ministries in the videos that accompany this book. We want to help you see what the Bible has to offer when it's read from a Wesleyan perspective. It's not the only way to read Scripture, but you'll find that it's true to the Bible, it's holistic in its approach, and, amazingly, it's perfectly suited to the twenty-first century.

When Christians were first identified as a separate group, they were called people who belonged to "the Way" (Acts 9:2). Christianity was understood to include a relationship to the risen Jesus, participation in a community, and a journey to salvation. When Paul described his whole life, he said, "I . . . have finished the race" (2 Timothy 4:7). The author of Hebrews exhorted people to a journey: "Let's also run the race that is set before us . . . and fix our eyes on Jesus, faith's pioneer and perfecter" (Hebrews 12:1-2). Following Jesus is a lifelong journey that can be described as a race, a pilgrimage, a way toward the Promised Land.

Of course, it's possible to make that journey without a map. Imagine getting in your car in Miami and trying to reach Seattle. Without a map or GPS, you could make the trip by trial and error. You could ask people for directions along the way. They might point you in the right direction, or they might send you on a detour. If you make the journey without a map, you might not reach your chosen destination. Or, if you do reach it, you might take such wide detours that the trip would take much longer than necessary. You might enjoy Portland, Maine or McAllen, Texas or San Diego, California, but visiting them would most certainly take longer than a more direct route. A map is an indispensable tool to use in planning your journey and making decisions along the way. It's helpful to know where you are and where you are going!

The Bible is our map, but it's old enough and complex enough that Christians have developed ways of reading it to guide believers on the journey. The Wesleyan Way of Christianity has its approach to understanding Scripture, and this study is in part a summary and exploration of that understanding.

I developed this study to help you find your life's goal. I believe God wants you to be saved from sin and delivered to a happy and whole life as one of Christ's disciples. That journey is so much easier if you open yourself to the Bible's teaching, if you listen to the wisdom of Christians who have traveled before you, and if you do it in community—with a group of fellow seekers or disciples who will support you, encourage you, and challenge you along the way. Ideally that community of sisters and brothers and friends will hold you accountable for becoming your best self. Our efforts to become the people we want to be are often done in groups, whether Alcoholics Anonymous, Weight Watchers, Walk to Emmaus, a women's Bible study, a men's group, or a Sunday school class. We need each other.

However, no book, no group, no church has all the answers. When you finish this study, you still will have questions and you still will be seeking to understand fully the amazing grace of God, the power of the Holy Spirit, and the deep joys of following Jesus.

I hope and pray that, along with a group of others who want to follow Jesus more fully, you will discover the Christian journey to be full of deep joy and meaning. That has been my experience—that following the Wesleyan Way has been an incredible blessing. I hope that you, too, are blessed by what you experience in this study.

1.

Following Christ
Is a Way of Life

What is the good life? How do you live well? Is it possible to be successful, joyful, or blessed? Does human life have a purpose? Can someone truly be happy? Is fulfillment possible?

Wesleyan Christians believe that following Jesus is the answer to all these questions, that following Jesus is the best way to live our lives with the maximum of meaning, purpose, and joy.

To some people, it's an outrageous claim. How can anyone dare to suggest that one way of life is best? To other people, especially those who have been Christians all their lives, it's obvious that following Jesus is the best way to live. But even those people sometimes wonder what following Jesus really means. If we truly followed Jesus with utmost seriousness and intentionality, what would it look like?

This study of the Wesleyan Way seeks to engage you in a conversation to help you answer that question. The conversation can be between you and me, among you and the video presenters, or with a group of people in your life who are journeying together.

The Wesleyan Way of salvation is an answer to questions about how to live well. It is an answer based on Scripture, summarizing the fundamental themes of the Bible and the life-shaping message of Jesus Christ. It can be summarized briefly like this:

God has a plan for every human being. Every person has been invited to receive God's help in achieving that goal. And though God may have a specific plan for one

God has a plan for every human being.

13

individual, the general plan that applies to you and every other person is this: God wants you to love God and your neighbor in all that you think, say, and do.

Jesus expressed the plan in a simple, compelling way. One of the religious scholars of his day, someone who had studied the biblical laws, asked Jesus a hotly debated question. The Jewish scholars knew that there were 613 commandments in the Torah, and they thought that obedience to the law was the way to please God and live a good life. So they asked him which one of all these commandments was most important. The conversation is found in Matthew 22:34-50:

> When the Pharisees heard that Jesus had left the Sadducees speechless, they met together. One of them, a legal expert, tested him. Teacher, what is the greatest commandment in the Law? He replied, "You must love the Lord your God with all your heart, with all your being, and with all your mind. This is the first and greatest commandment. And the second is like it: You must love your neighbor as you love yourself. All the Law and the Prophets depend on these two commands."

Jesus' first answer cited Deuteronomy 6:4-5. This was one of the usual answers; it was and is a prominent commandment among the Jewish community. But note that Jesus coupled his first answer with Leviticus 19:18, and he claimed that all the rest of the commandments depend on these two.

> **Salvation is a journey toward eternal happiness.**

This was Jesus' way of summarizing how God expects human beings to live.

We live in a world full of options. There are many different religions. There are many secular philosophies suggesting that having no religion is the best option. And there are many people who drift through life with no religion, no philosophy, and not much thought about the big questions such as "What is my purpose here on earth?"

The Wesleyan Way, in answering those questions, starts with Jesus' most important commandments—love of God and love of neighbor. And yet, we know that we aren't following those two commandments the way we should. All of us are sinners. How can we possibly reach the God-given goal of our lives? If we are honest with God and with ourselves, we have to admit that following Jesus is hard.

But following Jesus, regardless of its difficulty, is the best answer to life's important questions. The Wesleyan Way describes Christianity as a journey of following Jesus toward the goal of loving God with all of our heart, mind, soul, and strength and loving our neighbors as ourselves. Christianity is often described as salvation. In the Wesleyan Way, salvation is a journey toward eternal happiness.

Salvation Is Good News

The word *salvation* sometimes has been misused by Christians and misunderstood by others. Yet, as with many other words found in the Bible, it is best to keep using them and to do so with as much clarity as possible. When talking about the Wesleyan Way of salvation, one should keep in mind what Jesus said to many people whom he met. For many, salvation was about healing them of the brokenness in their lives. For some this meant physical healing. For others it was restoring broken relationships. For still others it meant life after death in paradise. One way of expressing this wide variety of meanings is to say that salvation is *from* all the bad things in life and *for* true happiness, joy, and truth.

Something Was Missing

I was not raised in church. Faith was just not part of our vocabulary. My sister and I were raised to go to school and value education and do well, which we did.

But I felt lost. I felt something was empty inside of me. Something was missing. And one of my friends said, "Andy, you're asking religious questions. You should start searching there."

I had a Roman Catholic girlfriend at that time, and I went to mass with her. God began to move, and I began to feel the Holy Spirit, and my heart started to change. Then once, in the middle of the night, I heard a voice: "If you will follow me, all your questions will be answered." I knew that was my moment. I said yes to Jesus that night, and I've never looked back.

To me, the life that matters is being connected to Jesus every minute of every day. Being connected means you're always thinking, What would Jesus have me do? Where is the Holy Spirit leading me right now? If you do that, you discover there are no ordinary moments. God is always trying to break in, and the more you look for it, the more you see him. He's alive. He's here. He wants to be known.

Andy Nixon
Lead Pastor, The Loft
The Woodlands United Methodist Church
The Woodlands, Texas

From *The Wesleyan Way* DVD

It doesn't help that at times salvation has been "dumbed down" to a series of partial meanings. Each meaning contains elements of truth but by itself is inadequate. Let's look at a few of these partial meanings.

Salvation is more than a one-time "getting saved" experience, though that may represent an important moment on the journey. The revival and camp-meeting traditions in Protestant Christianity have placed a strong emphasis on the initial commitment of one's life to Christ as Lord and Savior. Many people tell stories of dramatic conversions, in which suddenly they felt the Lord forgiving their sins and accepting them as a beloved child. Some of our most powerful hymns were written to express the longing sinners have for that experience, such as "Alas! and Did My Savior Bleed":

> At the cross, at the cross, where I first saw the light
> And the burden of my heart rolled away
> It was there by faith I received my sight
> And now I am happy all the day.[1]

Some Christian traditions presume that everyone will have an experience like this. When people ask, "Are you saved?" they sometimes expect that you can identify the date and time when Christ came to you. They refer to the experience as being "born again." The Wesleyan Way can include being born again at an identifiable instant, but it also describes a variety of valid paths to Jesus. People have different ways of coming to faith, including being raised in the faith from infant baptism on and never leaving it. It can be a story of dramatic inspiration or gradual growth.

Salvation is also more than membership in a church, though church membership is part of it. In some cases church membership doesn't appear to be much different from any other group affiliation or even a club membership. Churches, like clubs, have a purpose, attendance expectations, dues and requirements, and benefits that go along with membership. Some congregations have boiled down their understanding of salvation to "join our club—see what great benefits we offer!"

Salvation is more than a family affiliation, though one's family and upbringing may influence our path. There is no doubt that our families shape many things about us. Some of those things are genetic. Others involve a complex web of relationships, values, and loyalties that constitute a family's identity. Thus, because religion is an expression of our highest and most sacred values and relationships, our families often shape our faith. In more traditional societies, one's experience of salvation is actually part of the family experience, and changing religions is unheard of.

My own experience was not of changing religions but of going deeper into my own faith. I am a fourth-generation Methodist and United Methodist pastor. For a year and a half, I did not attend church and did not have a personal faith in Christ. I had been through confirmation and was a member of a local United Methodist Church, but I had drifted from Christ and did not know him as Lord and Savior of my life. At the same time, I was active in various United Methodist activities focused on peace, justice, and helping the poor. While at college I started a spiritual journey that led me to salvation. It was done in the Wesleyan Way, and I claimed a saving relationship with Christ that was expressed in my United Methodist roots more deeply than ever before.

For some of you, finding Christ may mean rejecting some of your family's values or traditions. Whatever one's starting point, it's clear that salvation is more than one's family affiliation.

Either way, salvation is a lifelong journey. Once someone has entered into the Christian life, they have been saved but are still being saved. Christians should understand that God has not finished with them just because they entered into a saving relationship. All of us are sinners, and it takes a lifetime to become the kind of people God intends us to be.

> There is both unity and diversity among the followers of Jesus.

Salvation is holistic and long-term, not partial or short-term. It is a way of life that shapes everything we think, everything we do, everything we are. It shapes our relationships and the ways we spend our time, money, and energy. It is all-encompassing, because the God who created the universe and loves it passionately deserves nothing less.

The Wesleyan Way of salvation does not make us identical copies of each other. Though the way itself is the same for all, each of us makes the journey at our own pace, with our own abilities, and in our own style. There is both unity and diversity among the followers of Jesus.

The Wesleyan Way Brings the Bible's Message to Life

Where did the Wesleyan Way come from? It is based on the Bible. The Bible is a complex collection of sixty-six books, and the Roman Catholic version has extra books that Protestants call the Apocrypha. The Bible has a wide variety of literature types, from poetry to history to letters to Gospels to apocalyptic prophecy. Scripture is authoritative for all Christians, but the differences within the Christian family show that we read this amazing, complex, and powerful book in different ways. Each way of reading Scripture can lead to a different version of the Christian life.

The Wesleyan Way of reading and interpreting the Bible avoids some of the most contentious and divisive issues among Christians and focuses on the basic message of the text. It is the way John Wesley and his followers have read Scripture since the 1700s. Wesley himself said that the Wesleyan Way is nothing new; it is "the old religion, the religion of the Bible, the religion of the [early] Church, the religion of the Church of England."[2] Wesley himself believed that Christians all too often did not follow the way. In fact, he said the greatest obstacle to the spread of Christianity was (and is) the behavior of Christians.

One of the ironies of Wesleyan Christianity is that, in many cases, the Wesleyan Way is not practiced adequately by those who belong to churches in the Wesleyan tradition, such as Methodist, Nazarene, and Pentecostal denominations. One reason for engaging in this study is to recommit to our highest and best values as followers of Jesus. Another reason is to invite those who are not yet followers of Jesus to consider beginning the journey.

What we will study in this book and DVD is the Wesleyan Way of following Jesus, as taught by John and Charles Wesley in their eighteenth-century movement. That movement sought the renewal of their church, the Church of England, but it eventually led to the formation of many different Wesleyan churches. The Wesleyan Way presented in this study relates to the official teaching of many of those groups. Those of us in the Wesleyan tradition don't always practice this way of life very well, but if you ask and look carefully, this is what we are trying to do when we are at our best.

> *Wesleyans believe in the authority of the Bible.*

Wesleyans believe in the authority of the Bible. We know that the Holy Scripture is complex and has many parts that address a wide variety of topics and concerns. Those of us following the Wesleyan Way believe that the Bible is the inspired Word of God, communicated through human beings and reflecting their languages, cultures, and times in which they lived. As a result, Scripture should be understood in the light of its original context. One Wesleyan denomination expresses it this way in their Confession of Faith:

> We believe the Holy Bible, Old and New Testaments, reveals the Word of God so far as it is necessary for our salvation. It is to be received through the Holy Spirit as the true rule and guide for faith and practice. Whatever is not revealed in or established by the Holy Scriptures is not to be made an article of faith nor is it to be taught as essential to salvation.[3]

Though some Christians teach that the Bible is without error of any kind, Wesleyans believe it to be trustworthy in all matters relating to our faith. Thus, Wesleyans do not spend much time worrying about predicting when the world will end based on the visions of Daniel or the Book of Revelation, and we are willing to accept modern science's finding that the universe is billions of years old. Instead, we try to focus on what we believe to be the main message of Scripture: the way of salvation.

John Wesley believed that the way of salvation is the main theme that ties together the whole of the Bible. That theme is expressed in the story of a God who created humanity in his own image. When humanity sinned and became separated from God, God continued to love his creation and to seek the redemption of the human race, giving Israel the law and sending prophets to teach the people. In the fullness of time, God sent his Son to teach and then die for the sins of the world. God's saving grace was then offered to all humanity through the preaching of the gospel. We are saved by God's grace through faith in Christ, which comes to us in the form of "prevenient" or preparing grace, "justifying" or accepting grace, and "sanctifying" or sustaining grace.

The gospel is good news. The very word *gospel* is a shortened form of the older English words "good spell" or "good news." Going back to the Greek language in which the New Testament was written, each of the first four books was the *euangelion* according to its author—Matthew, Mark, Luke, or John. The prefix *eu* means "good" and *angelion* means "news" (and is related to the word *angel*, which means "messenger"). Thus, the gospel is a book about the good news God is sending into the world in the birth, life, death, and resurrection of Jesus Christ. Christ is the bearer of God's grace to a world that desperately needs to be loved.

For people such as you and me, who are aware that they are broken and that life offers more than they are currently experiencing, the opportunity to heal our brokenness and find a way to fulfillment is great news!

If you'd like more detailed information about Wesleyan Christianity, including some writings of John Wesley and hymns of Charles Wesley, go the study's website, www.TheWesleyanWay.com.

Salvation Is a Journey

The Wesleyan Way is the journey of a lifetime.

From one point of view, it's a journey with a destination called eternal life. Wesleyan Christians believe that after we die, we go to live forever with God. Christ looked at the criminal crucified with him and said "I assure you that today you will be with me in paradise" (Luke 23:43).

At the same time, we believe that eternal life is a quality of life lived here on earth. In the Sermon on the Mount in Matthew 5–7, Jesus gave us a series of statements called the Beatitudes. Nine of these statements begin with a word normally translated as "blessed" so that, for example, it reads "Blessed are the poor in spirit, for theirs is the kingdom of heaven" (NRSV). John Wesley translated the word as "happy" so that it reads "Happy are the poor in spirit, for theirs is the kingdom of heaven." Wesley knew the Bible was teaching us that genuine happiness comes from following Jesus.

The ultimate goal of following Jesus is life forever with God. The short-term goal (the length of our lives here on earth) is having a life that matters. The Wesleyan Way teaches that God has created each person to live in relationship with him. People are happiest and most fulfilled when they acknowledge God as creator and Lord and when they seek to be the kind of men and women God intended.

This way of life has a beginning and a direction toward an end. Like many journeys, it may also have detours and some obstacles along the way. It is often difficult, but it also has surprises and amazingly beautiful moments. The journey has five stages:

1. Creation in God's image

You are special.

2. Sin

We all have issues.

3. Repentance

You can turn your life around with God's help.

4. Justification

God will accept you by grace through faith.

5. Sanctification

You can become like Jesus by grace through faith.

This study will describe each of those stages and how the Wesleyan Way helps people make that journey. The power of God's grace is real, and the journey is possible with God's help. Living a life that matters is one of the goals of following the Wesleyan Way, and inviting others to make the journey with us is part of it. We know that the way will be hard at times, but a relationship with Christ provides the strength and resources to live a blessed life regardless of bumps in the road or unexpected detours.

This chapter describes the Wesleyan Way of salvation in general terms as a way of life that leads to the deepest possible joys. In chapter 2 we focus on who God is and God's intentions for creation. Knowing that the power of love pervades the universe can change our outlook on everything! In chapter 3 we acknowledge the goodness of creation as well as the reality of sin. Sin is a disease for which salvation is the cure. Chapter 4 talks about turning one's life toward God. People's lives can be headed in many different directions, and turning toward God is the starting point of the Wesleyan Way. In chapter 5 we acknowledge that God's power through grace and the Christian community are essential aspects of the journey. Chapter 6 reminds us that the goal of the journey is to transform oneself and the world to be more in line with God's intentions for us. Along the way, we should share the good news of what we have found with others, as described in chapter 7. Chapter 8 talks about the obstacles that will inevitably arise and how a life in Christ can triumph even over death.

The key insight of this program is that salvation is lifelong process. There are people who talk about the Christian faith as if it were an instantaneous single event. They are right to point out that, on occasion, a single moment can be a dramatic and life-changing turning point. But in the Wesleyan Way, following Christ takes a lifetime, and any single turning point is then followed by years of going in the new direction.

Following Jesus is all about a relationship with him, and all relationships are complicated. Think about being a parent and about all the skills needed to be a good father or mother. Sometimes one needs to be a provider, earning money and then arranging for food, clothing, and shelter. Sometimes one needs to be a caregiver in times of illness. Sometimes one is a teacher, helping the child learn to read, to avoid danger, and to adopt positive values. Sometimes one is a coach, giving advice and helping the child figure out what to do. Sometimes one is a disciplinarian, doling out punishments and rewards.

In the same way, following Jesus has many aspects. Part of discipleship is our beliefs, or what we think is true about God, the world, and humanity. Part of discipleship is our behavior, always trying to do good. Part of discipleship is practicing spiritual disciplines such as prayer, worship, Bible study, and Holy Communion. Part of discipleship is being baptized into the body of Christ and participating as a member of Christ's church. Part of discipleship is discovering spiritual gifts and then using them in service for Christ. Part of discipleship is sharing faith with those who don't know Christ as Lord and Savior.

The good news is that we don't make the Christian journey alone.

Meaning, purpose, and joy are best experienced by following Jesus Christ as Lord and Savior. Christians have a vision of how to live that is described as discipleship.

We Journey Together as God's Church

The good news is that we don't make the Christian journey alone. Becoming a disciple of Jesus means that you join a community of people who are on the same path. Jesus modeled this by forming a close-knit body of followers. They were led by the twelve disciples, but the group was much larger than that.

Following Jesus means participating in a Christian community, usually a church. Many people criticize organized religion, saying that churches fail to live up their high calling and that one can be a Christian without participating in any church. For Wesleyans, this is a deep misunderstanding of what it means to follow Jesus. We can be interested in Jesus, attracted to Jesus, or curious about Jesus without belonging to a church. We can agree with Jesus about some of his ideas. We can appreciate Jesus as a significant historical figure. But these steps aren't enough to make us disciples of Jesus.

Discipleship requires a commitment deeper than just curiosity or agreement. It requires accepting Christ on his own terms as the incarnate Son of God and savior of the world. It requires baptism and participation in Christ's church. It requires sacrifice and service to God and to one's neighbor. In short, being a disciple is a way of life.

We know that all Christian churches are imperfect. Like the believers who form their congregations, they sometimes focus on themselves rather than on God. They sometimes treat people inappropriately, and they sometimes preach and teach false doctrines. Yet Jesus accepted the twelve as his disciples despite their shortcomings. God has decided to use a less-than-perfect church to accomplish God's purposes.

We Sing the Faith on the Journey

The love we experience with God and each other is a little bit of heaven in this life.

Charles Wesley preached and taught beside his brother John. He made many contributions to the Wesleyan Way, but no contributions were more important than his hymns. He wrote more than six thousand of them! Ever since, Wesleyans have sung about their faith, using the hymns of Charles Wesley and others. Hymns have expressed their beliefs, offered prayers and praise to God, and told stories about faith journeys. You could describe the entire Wesleyan Way of salvation by paying close attention to these hymns. In each chapter of this book I will introduce a hymn that embodies a key learning from that chapter.

In the spring of 1738, soon after John and Charles Wesley had returned from a less-than-successful trip to the Georgia Colony in America, they were talking with a friend about their Christian faith. John and Charles were struggling to decide whether or not they truly were saved (please note that both Charles and John were ordained ministers of the Church of England at the time!), and their friend was giving them advice. In the middle of the conversation, Charles exclaimed, "How I wish I had a thousand tongues to praise my God!"

This spontaneous outburst was the inspiration for a poem, which one year later Charles incorporated into a hymn, one of the most important and famous of the many he wrote. In the hymn, he starts out praising God and wishing for greater capacity to honor the God who saved him. God is our creator and our redeemer. He actively helps those in need. He forgives the sinner. He helps the blind to see. He makes the lame to walk.

When we sing the hymn, we are acknowledging a relationship to God that starts with praise for who God is. God is truly glorious and is acting in the world in ways that make a difference. We are also acknowledging who we are and what we believe. In Christ we know God and know that our sins are forgiven. We anticipate heaven, and we believe that the love we experience with God and each other is a little bit of heaven in this life.

"O For a Thousand Tongues to Sing"

Charles Wesley's hymn expresses the deep conviction that there is a God, and this God is in the business of saving the world. God cancels sin and its power. God takes depressed people and gives them joy. God helps the lame to walk and the blind to see. We not only praise this God for his love and all he has done but also we tell others about him using as many tongues as we can muster.

TRADITIONAL	CONTEMPORARY REPHRASING
O for a thousand tongues to sing My great Redeemer's praise The glories of my God and King The triumphs of his grace! . . .	O, that my one voice could sound like a choir of thousands, singing the praises of my great Redeemer, the glories of my God, my King, singing his victories and his grace! . . .
He breaks the power of canceled sin He sets the prisoner free; His blood can make the foulest clean; His blood availed for me.	Our sin is gone and has no power over us; no, Jesus set us free from that prison. The blood of his death washes snowy white the dirtiest among us. His blood saves even me.
He speaks, and listening to his voice, New life the dead receive; The mournful, broken hearts rejoice, The humble poor believe.	When Jesus speaks, anyone who hears him receives a fresh start, a new life. Broken hearts find joy and are happy. The humble and poor believe.
Hear him, ye deaf; his praise, ye dumb, Your loosened tongues employ; Ye blind behold your Savior come, And leap, ye lame, for joy.	Hard of hearing? Listen and hear his voice. Can't speak? Shout his praises. Can't see? Look, behold the face of your Savior. Can't walk? Jump for joy!
In Christ, your head, you then shall know, Shall feel your sins forgiven; Anticipate your heaven below, And own that love is heaven.[4]	When Christ is number one in your life, you know it, you feel it—forgiveness! On earth, we eagerly await our future in heaven, but we know heaven on earth when we love God and love one another.

2.

Love Ultimately Wins

All of us have to decide the religious question for ourselves: Who or what ultimately matters in the universe? We might express this question about ultimate reality as four religious questions:

- Is there a God?
- If so, who is God?
- Does human life have a purpose?
- If so, what is it?

The history of religions is filled with many different answers to these questions. Some religions have worshipped multiple gods and goddesses. Within Western culture, we are perhaps most familiar with the Greek pantheon of Zeus, Hera, Athena, Hermes, Poseidon, Ares, and others. In Roman religion each of the Greek deities was given a different name. Hinduism and ancient Egyptian religion also worshipped multiple deities.

Judaism stood out from other religious groups in its insistence that there was only one god and they could only worship the Lord. Judaism, with Christianity and Islam following after, held the belief that this one God had revealed himself to Abraham and then had delivered a revelation to Moses and the prophets. When God first spoke to Moses out of the burning bush, he said, "I am the God of your father, the God of Abraham, the God of Isaac, and the God of Jacob." Today Christians refer to this same God as the one whom Jesus called "Father" and who inspired the writers of the Bible.

Answering the questions "Is there a God?" and "Who is God?" makes it easier to draw some conclusions about the meaning and purpose of human life. If there is a supreme being who either made the world or controls it, then our place in the universe as humans becomes clearer. If there is no God and the universe is a cosmic accident, then some other biologically driven purpose might be proposed. Some have said we are wired for survival of our species and that is the highest good. Various religions suggest that pleasing or fulfilling the intention of a supreme being is the answer.

How do we settle these questions?

Within the Christian tradition, theologians and philosophers have sometimes offered arguments to prove the existence of God. Thomas Aquinas, teaching in thirteenth-century Paris, offered five proofs for the existence of God. Several of these are still offered today in various forms, as people seek to prove God's existence. Anselm of Canterbury offered another proof, writing that God is that "than which no greater can be conceived." Then, Anselm reasoned, that than which no greater can be conceived must exist. Therefore God must exist.[5] A few modern philosophers have shown interest in Anselm's proposal.

My experience is that no one has ever been converted to Christianity by an argument. Rather, the arguments of theologians and philosophers seem most useful after the fact, showing that the faith commitments of believers do in fact make sense and are rationally defensible.

The Bible itself never offers any proof for the existence of God. Instead, its opening verse assumes there is a God and describes what that God has done. "When God began to create the heavens and the earth . . ." (Genesis 1:1).

For Christians, the answer to the four religious questions is ultimately settled by faith—a commitment to live in this way because it fits. It makes sense. It is right. According to Hebrews 11:1, "Faith is the reality of what we hope for, the proof of what we don't see." Faith is our decision that God is real and that we want to live our lives in relationship with God. To put it another way: God is love, and love ultimately wins.

> *God is love, and love ultimately wins.*

God Is Love

The conviction that God is love runs through the whole of the Bible:

- Genesis 1—A loving God creates the world out of nothing and calls it good.
- Exodus 3:7—A loving God hears the cry of his people in slavery and delivers them through the leadership of Moses.
- Exodus 20:6—In the Ten Commandments, God describes himself as showing steadfast love to all who love him.
- Psalms—Fifty of the Psalms praise God for steadfast love. Psalm 136 (NRSV) closes each of its twenty-six verses with the words "for his steadfast love endures forever."

- John 3:16—Describes the coming of Christ as an action based on God's love for the world.
- 1 John 4:8—Summarizes God's very being as love.

There are many things that can be said about God's nature and being. Philosophers and theologians often speak of God's attributes, using adjectives such as the following:

Omnipresent—God is everywhere.

Omnipotent—God is all-powerful.

A Life of Love

People don't come to faith in Christ because of our superior theological arguments. They come to faith in Christ because somebody cares about them. They think, Okay, it's great to have money and a nice car and a house at the lake, but what I really want is to know that somebody notices, somebody cares. We have a deep need for unconditional love. We need to know our lives have meaning and purpose. We need grace. We need to feel there's a chance for a new beginning and a fresh start. We need to feel we're not alone. And we need to feel that in the darkest moments of our lives, there's always hope.

God is love. We are meant to live a life of love, to love God with all our heart and to love our neighbors as we love ourselves. And that love isn't a warm mushy feeling. It's an action, a way of putting the needs of another before myself. It's being concerned, wanting to bless and build up and encourage somebody else. It's thinking of what's best for you before I think of what's best for me.

When Christians actually live that way instead of judging and pointing our fingers, the hardest of hearts become responsive and the world is changed.

Adam Hamilton
Senior Pastor
The United Methodist Church of the Resurrection
Leawood, Kansas

From *The Wesleyan Way* DVD

Omniscient—God is all-knowing.

Sovereign—God rules the universe.

Eternal—God has always existed, will never cease to exist, and is not subject
to time.

Wise—God knows the right thing to do.

Holy—God is completely other and completely righteous

John Wesley believed all these attributes to be true, but he regarded God's most important attribute—indeed, God's very definition—to be love. Wesley wrote:

God is often styled holy, righteous, wise; but not holiness, righteousness, or wisdom in the abstract, as he is said to be love; intimating that this is his darling, his reigning attribute, the attribute that sheds an amiable glory on all his other perfections.[6]

Charles Wesley expressed the same thought in a powerful hymn, "Love Divine, All Loves Excelling," written as a prayer, in which he addressed God as love itself:

Love Divine, all loves excelling,
Joy of heaven to earth come down;
Fix in us thy humble dwelling;
All thy faithful mercies crown!
Jesus, thou art all compassion,
Pure, unbounded love thou art;
Visit us with thy salvation;
Enter every trembling heart.[7]

God Is One God in Three Persons

When Scripture is taken as a whole, both Old and New Testaments, and one seeks to form a comprehensive account of God's nature and activity, Wesleyans believe that God is love.

The description of God as a Trinity—one God in three persons—was not totally clear until Christ came. There were hints in the Old Testament. In Genesis 1:26 the God says, "Let us make humanity in our image to resemble us so that they may take charge of the fish of the sea, the birds of the sky, the livestock, all the earth, and all the crawling things on earth." The pronoun for God and the verb are unmistakably plural. In many places God's Spirit is referenced, including Psalm 139:7

which says, "Where could I go to get away from your spirit? Where could I go to escape your presence?"

Yet the crucial step in the development of human understanding about the Trinity came with the revelation that Jesus truly is God. This revelation came to Jewish followers of Jesus who knew Deuteronomy 6:4 by heart. They knew there was just one God, yet they were convinced that Jesus was also God. John's Gospel uses a technical term from Greek philosophy to explain how this could be. Philosophers had said that there was a *logos*, a word, that was part of the divine nature. John goes on to make the extraordinary claim that distinguished the Christians from other believers in the oneness of God: this Word became flesh and dwelt among us.

This word became flesh and dwelt among us.

The word *trinity* does not appear in Scripture, but as we have seen, all the component parts of this doctrine are present. The church struggled for a long time to get the right words to express what the Bible was teaching. In A.D. 325, a council of bishops meeting in Nicaea developed the language that God is one being but has always existed in three persons. The first part of the Nicene Creed says this:

> We believe in one God, the Father, the Almighty, maker of heaven and earth, of all that is, seen and unseen. We believe in one Lord, Jesus Christ, the only Son of God, eternally begotten of the Father, God from God, Light from Light, true God from true God, begotten, not made, of one Being with the Father; through him all things were made.[8]

This is the defining expression of our understanding of God's triune or three-part nature. There is one God who is Father, Son, and Holy Spirit. Let's take a look at those three parts and what Scripture tells us about them.

God Called Israel

God's call of Israel began with Abraham. God said to Abraham:

> "Leave your land, your family, and your father's household for the land that I will show you. I will make of you a great nation and will bless you. I will make your name respected, and you will be a blessing. I will bless those who bless you, those who curse you I will curse; all the families of earth will be blessed because of you."

This call began the special relationship that Abraham's descendants have had with God ever since. Abraham's son Isaac had a son named Jacob. After wrestling with God at the river Jabbok, Jacob was renamed Israel and his descendants were called

Israelites. They went to Egypt and lived there for many years, ending up in slavery to the Egyptians.

The Exodus from slavery in Egypt was a defining moment for the Israelites. The Passover recalls God's miraculous actions to save them: God remembered his people and brought them out of slavery on a journey to a land of their own.

At Mount Sinai, God gave the law to the people of Israel and commanded them to obey. For Jews, the law comprises the first five books of the Bible. One of its most important verses is Deuteronomy 6:4-5 which says, "Hear, O Israel: The LORD is our God, the LORD alone. You shall love the LORD your God with all your heart, and with all your soul, and with all your might" (NRSV).

> Despite the Israelites' misbehavior, God did not forsake them.

Despite the Israelites' misbehavior over many generations, God did not forsake them. He rescued them from slavery in the Exodus. He gave them a land "flowing with milk and honey." When they worshipped other gods, borrowing the practices of neighboring peoples, he sent them prophets to remind them that God wished them to be a holy people.

Part of their holiness was worshipping the Lord and only him. Another part was how they treated the poor, especially widows and orphans, who were the most vulnerable. The Israelites insisted that foreigners be welcomed and treated fairly. The prophets kept them focused on worship of the Lord and justice for all. Some of the prophets also looked forward to a future king of Israel who would redeem his people. Many passages from Isaiah and Malachi were later interpreted to be foretelling a Messiah.

The destruction of the Temple in Jerusalem and subsequent exile of key leaders to Babylon was another defining time in the Israelites' relationship with God. They had to learn that God was truly universal and not limited to the Temple in Jerusalem or the land of Israel. Some scholars believe this to be the time when Jews developed patterns of worshipping God in synagogues. When the Babylonians were conquered by the Persians, the key leaders of Israel were allowed to return to Jerusalem and build a new Temple.

Until modern times, the Jews were ruled by one empire after another. The hope for a Messiah to free the people and rule over the nation grew as time went on.

God Sent His Son

If you have ever wondered why we refer to our years as "AD," you'll be interested to know that it stands for the Latin *anno domini* or "year of our Lord." That is because Christians believe that the birth of Christ is the turning point of all human history and therefore that time should be measured before and after Christ was born.

When the great event happened, the angels told the shepherds, "Do not be afraid; for see—I am bringing you good news of great joy for all the people: to you is born this day in the city of David a Savior, who is the Messiah, the Lord" (Luke 2:10-11 NRSV). The word *messiah* in Hebrew means "anointed" and typically refers to the anointing of the King of Israel, as Samuel anointed David in 1 Samuel 16:13. The angels were telling the shepherds that a new king of Israel had been born.

Through all his miracles and teachings, Jesus' disciples gradually came to believe that he indeed was the Messiah. When Jesus asked them, "Who do you say that I am?" Simon Peter answered, "You are the Messiah, the Son of the living God." Jesus responded, "Blessed are you, Simon son of Jonah! For flesh and blood has not revealed this to you, but my Father in heaven" (Matthew 16:16-17 NRSV). John's Gospel records Jesus as twice saying that he and the Father are one (John 10:30, 17:11). In the closing verses of Matthew's Gospel, Jesus commands the disciples to baptize "in the name of the Father and of the Son and of the Holy Spirit" (Matthew 28:19).

Though God's three parts are one, in some sense there clearly is a difference between God the Father and Jesus. Regarding the time when the world will come to an end Jesus said, "But nobody knows when that day or hour will come, not the heavenly angels and not the Son. Only the Father knows" (Matthew 24:36). In the Garden of Gethsemane, just before he was arrested and crucified, Jesus prayed, "My Father, if it's possible, take this cup of suffering away from me. However—not what I want but what you want" (Matthew 27:46). And while hanging on the cross he cried, "My God, my God, why have you left me?" (Matthew 27:46).These three texts clearly indicate that God the Father knows things and wills things that Jesus does not share.

The disciples saw the risen Christ on Easter Sunday, then came to believe that Jesus' death and resurrection fulfilled the prophecies of the Old Testament, especially the "suffering servant" passages of Isaiah 53:4-6:

> It was certainly our sickness that he carried, and our sufferings that he bore,
> but we thought him afflicted, struck down by God and tormented. He was
> pierced because of our rebellions and crushed because of our crimes. He bore
> the punishment that made us whole; by his wounds we are healed. Like sheep
> we had all wandered away, each going its own way, but the LORD let fall on
> him all our crimes.

Luke relates how the risen Christ on Easter Sunday appeared to two disciples and explained why the Messiah had to die. He was then revealed to them in the breaking of bread at Emmaus. (Luke 24:25-31).

God Sent the Holy Spirit

Jesus promised that after he ascended to the Father, God would not leave the disciples orphaned. God would send another advocate. Jesus said, "And I will ask the Father, and he will give you another Advocate, to be with you forever. This is the Spirit of truth, whom the world cannot receive, because it neither sees him nor knows him. You know him, because he abides with you, and he will be in you" (John 14:16-17 NRSV) The Book of Acts has Jesus making a similar promise right before his ascension, that the disciples would receive power when the Holy Spirit came upon them. This promise was fulfilled on the day of Pentecost when the Holy Spirit was given to the disciples (Acts 1–2).

Receiving the Holy Spirit was a sign that God continued to empower the disciples so they could be witnesses of the risen Christ. When Gentiles received the Spirit, Peter was moved to claim that even they could become disciples of Christ without having to follow the ceremonial parts of the Old Testament law. This was a very contentious question, whether Gentiles had to become Jews first before becoming Christians. In Acts 15 the leaders met in a Council at Jerusalem and debated the question. At the end, they sent a letter to the Christian communities, which said, "The Holy Spirit has led us to the decision that no burden should be placed on you other than these essentials . . ." (Acts 15:28). Wesleyans believe that the Holy Spirit continues to be present in the church today. Every time I preach, right before the sermon I pray, "Almighty God, we thank you for the presence of the Holy Spirit in this place, for we trust your promise that where two or three are gathered, there you will be also." I then ask for the congregation to be given eyes, ears, hands, and feet to know God's presence and to do his will. We believe the Holy Spirit is experienced in a variety of ways. Some Wesleyans worship in the Pentecostal tradition with loud music, healing, speaking in tongues, shouting "Amen" and "Hallelujah" and other passionate expressions of faith. Others experience the Spirit as a "gentle whisper," as did the prophet Elijah (1 Kings 19:12 NIV).

God Is Not Male

Throughout the Bible, God is referred to as "he" when a pronoun must be used. Ancient Hebrew, Aramaic, and Greek, as well as modern languages, lack a pronoun making it clear that the one being referred to is a person but could be of either gender. Because of male dominance in the cultures in which Scripture was written, God has been referred to predominantly with masculine imagery and words.

Those who follow the Wesleyan Way, as well as most theologians, are clear that God is neither male nor female and that our calling God "Father" or "he" is primarily a way of emphasizing God's personal nature rather than God's gender. Thus, many persons who are sensitive to inclusive language go to great lengths to avoid masculine language for God. The result is, in one respect, a more accurate portrayal of God. At the same time, this more accurate portrayal loses touch with the language that Christ used to talk about the first person of the Trinity. At other times the portrayal creates linguistic difficulties.

Many Christians have responded by adding images of God as mother based on biblical texts. In the hymn "Praise to the Lord, the Almighty" there are references to God as *Lord*, *King*, and *him*. But stanza 4 uses a feminine image:

> Praise to the Lord, who doth nourish thy life and restore thee,
> Fitting thee well for the tasks that are ever before thee.
> Then to thy need God as a mother doth speed
> Spreading the wings of grace o'er thee.[9]

This hymn makes clear reference to Jesus' lament over Jerusalem, when he said, "Jerusalem, Jerusalem! You who kill the prophets and stone those who were sent to you. How often I wanted to gather your people together, just as a hen gathers her chicks under her wings. But you didn't want that" (Matthew 23:37).

God Is Love

The coming of the Christ to be born as Jesus of Nazareth was the highest and best expression of God's essential nature. God is love. The love of God was expressed in the relationship among the persons of the Trinity before creation. The creation of the universe was an act of love. When Israel rebelled—like an unfaithful wife, according to the prophet Hosea—God did not give up on us. Christ showed his forgiveness, as to the tax collector Zacchaeus.

Part of Jesus' ministry was forming a new community of followers. Those who believed in him as the Messiah were brought into a new relationship with God the Father. Jesus' ministry was a boundary-crossing enterprise that reached out to those in the Jewish community who had been shunned—lepers, women, tax collectors—as well as to Gentiles such as the Roman centurion whose daughter he healed. Jesus loved everyone.

When the Holy Spirit revealed to Peter that Gentiles could be included in the community of disciples without becoming Jews first, it was just one more revelation in line with all that Jesus had done. John put it clearly: "God so loved the world that he gave his only Son, so that everyone who believes in him won't perish but will have eternal life" (John 3:16).

God Calls the Church to Love

We have seen that God's very nature is love. God loves the world and God calls all human beings to love him and their neighbor. When we are baptized, we are baptized into Christ, into one body. A key New Testament metaphor for the church is as the body of Christ. Thus, if God is love, and Christ is God, then the church is the love of Christ embodied in the world. At its best, the church is a place where the Holy Spirit is both present and seen to be present. It shows God's love in its daily life through its words and actions. It is a loving community.

The earliest generations of Christians were known as a community that practiced sacrificial love. In a letter to the emperor Hadrian, a Christian named Aristides described the community this way:

> They love one another, and from widows they do not turn away their esteem; and they deliver the orphan from him who treats him harshly. And he, who has, gives to him who has not, without boasting. And when they see a stranger, they take him in to their homes and rejoice over him as a very brother; for they do not call them brethren after the flesh, but brethren after the spirit and in God.[10]

At its best, the church continues to do these things today. Thousands of churches feed the poor, welcome strangers, and help those suffering from natural disasters.

Yet the church is composed of human beings who are sinners. We are all too familiar with the many ways we fall short of truly embodying God's love. Nevertheless, loving and acting on that love remain the church's purpose and calling from God.

"Maker in Whom We Live"

Charles Wesley wrote this hymn in a Trinitarian pattern, praising God for all that he has done. It invites us to praise God specifically for the many ways he has blessed creation.

TRADITIONAL

Maker, in whom we live, in whom we are and move,
the glory, power, and praise receive for thy creating love.
Let all the angel throng give thanks to God on high,
while earth repeats the joyful song and echoes to the sky.

Incarnate Deity, let all the ransomed race
render in thanks their lives to thee for thy redeeming grace.
The grace to sinners showed ye heavenly choirs proclaim,
and cry, "Salvation to our God, salvation to the Lamb!"

Spirit of Holiness, let all thy saints adore
thy sacred energy, and bless thine heart-renewing power.
Not angel tongues can tell thy love's ecstatic height,
the glorious joy unspeakable, the beatific sight.

Eternal, Triune God, let all the hosts above,
let all on earth below record and dwell upon thy love.
When heaven and earth are fled before thy glorious face,
sing all the saints thy love hath made thine everlasting praise.[11]

CONTEMPORARY REPHRASING

God, you made us. We live and are and move in you.
Hear the praises and the glories for your creative and creating love.
Hear all the angels sing your praise
and we, here on earth, will echo back their song.

God, who came down to be one of us, we, for whom you gave your life as ransom,
give you our whole lives as an offering of thanks for your saving grace.
You showed us what grace is and so we sing with all the angels,
"God is the author of salvation!"

Holy Spirit, move in us to praise you
for your strength and power at work within us.
Even the angels fall short to speak about the heights of your great love,
your indescribable joy, your incomparable beauty.

Three-in-One God, Father, Spirit, Son, who was and is and is to come,
all the angels in heaven and all your creatures on earth remember and think about your love.
And on that day, when everything you made in heaven and on earth are set out before you as one big choir,
we'll sing together of your love and praise you forever and ever.

3.

It's a Good World
with Issues

The universe is full of beautiful and amazing sights. From the galaxies revealed by the Hubble Space Telescope to amazing forms of microscopic life, from the beauty of the prairie at sunset to the majesty of snow-covered mountains, from the magnificence of lions and elephants to the soft gentleness of a puppy dog—the world as we know it is a good creation.

One of the strongest philosophical arguments for the existence of God is called the argument from design—that such an amazing universe with all its complexity, beauty, and intricacy must have been planned by a supreme being. Genesis gives us two accounts of that creation and says that God was the creator. In Chapter 1, God creates the universe in six days. Six times God says that the creation is good.

For many years now, Wesleyans have been willing to accept modern scientific theories of evolution and geological change while at the same time accepting the truth of Scripture. The Wesleyan Way is faithful to Scripture by focusing on three primary messages of Genesis 1.

The first primary message is that God is the creator, and he created out of nothing. Modern physics postulates a "big bang," which began the universe but has no answer for what caused the creative process. Christian faith says that God caused the big bang. The ancient reference to six days was a metaphor that laid the basis for keeping the Sabbath day holy.

The second primary message is the goodness of creation. God knew what he was doing, and Christians should welcome all that God has created as having its own place

> Six times God says that the creation is good.

in the providential plan. Recent years have seen more frequent use of the scientific term *ecology*, which describes interrelated systems that make up the natural world and includes humans as one part of this complex system. Human impact on the atmosphere and water through pollution and the release of carbon has raised great concerns about protecting the environment. Such environmental concerns are clearly related to God's concern for his creation. God's love for the world is not simply for humanity, but for all creatures.

We Are Made in God's Image—All of Us!

The third primary message of Genesis 1 is humanity's special place in God's creation. According to the Bible, humanity is created in the image of God.

> Then God said, "Let us make humanity in our image to resemble us so that they may take charge of the fish of the sea, the birds of the sky, the livestock, all the earth, and all the crawling things on earth." God created humanity in God's own image, in the divine image God created them, male and female God created them. (Genesis 1:26-27)

An important point to notice in this key text is that both male and female were created in God's image, which again makes the point that God is beyond gender.

When Wesleyans discuss humanity, we talk about three different ways in which we are created in God's image. The first is that, like God, we are a spirit. There are those who wish to treat humanity as more closely related to the other animals, but Christianity puts us just a little below God. Psalm 8:3-9 expresses this anthropology beautifully:

> When I look up at your skies, at what your fingers made—the moon and the stars that you set firmly in place—what are human beings that you pay attention to them? You've made them only slightly less than divine, crowning them with glory and grandeur. You've let them rule over your handiwork, putting everything under their feet—all sheep and all cattle, the wild animals too, the birds in the sky, the fish of the ocean, everything that travels the pathways of the sea. LORD, our Lord, how majestic is your name throughout the earth!

Thus, while human beings may share many physical characteristics with animals, we are primarily spirits like God.

The second way we are created in God's image is also expressed in Psalm 8 and Genesis 1. God gave humanity dominion over the earth and its creatures. This is a huge responsibility! As our numbers have increased, our impact on the earth has increased and not always for the better. We have the opportunity to do a better job of caring for the world God loves, and our actions as Christians should always take environmental concerns into account. We are responsible.

The third and most important aspect of our being created in the image of God is that we are capable of love. God is love, and we were created with the purpose of loving

---

The Hands and Feet of Christ

Christianity is bigger than a Sunday morning experience. It's about being the hands and feet of Christ throughout the day, throughout the week. Whether it's through Habitat for Humanity or a community park cleanup, people want to join a movement that's about helping other people and being with folks in a time of need.

What drives me is the experience of growing up in my hometown. Walking out my door, my grandmother lived to the left, my great aunt and uncle to the right. Next to them was an older adult named Mr. George, who was born in 1899 and lived until I was in college. Across from him, we would pass by Mr. Pete Buckley's house on our bicycles. And so that was the village experience that I grew up in.

It gave me great admiration for those around me who may not have had all the resources and amenities, and yet they still had great character and work ethic and wanted to make sure that others had the resources that should be available to all people.

Some people say if I'm first, I'm the best. But in the faith community, the best is the one who's the greatest servant. All of us are created in the image of God, and we all have the love of God and a savior named Christ. And how we treat each other shows how seriously we take our faith and our walk with Jesus Christ.

Olu Brown
Lead Pastor
Impact United Methodist Church
Atlanta, Georgia

From *The Wesleyan Way* DVD

God and loving our neighbor as ourselves. When human beings are at our best, we love the Lord and each other.

One important side note is that we have just answered one of the key questions with which this study began. At the beginning of chapter 1 we asked, "Does human life have a purpose?" The Wesleyan Way answers yes, that we live the way God intended us to live. We live a life of love.

Human Rights, Diversity, and Environmental Justice

If humans are created in God's image, then every person is valuable in God's sight. The Old Testament commanded that the people of God should care for the poor, especially the widows and orphans who were the most vulnerable in society, and should welcome the alien and stranger into their communities.

Our care for the poor has developed into a commitment to human rights and human dignity, including our evolving commitment to the rights of women, who frequently have been subjected to discrimination and unequal treatment. Even parts of the Bible, reflecting the culture of the time in which it was written, have been used to violate the basic principle that all people are created in God's image.

A key example of our commitment to human rights is the fight against slavery. Though slavery has been practiced in many cultures, it was Europeans who developed a comprehensive theory of racial superiority that claimed to justify the enslavement of black people. For whites settling the continent of North America, there were powerful economic incentives for this type of mistreatment. Beginning in the eighteenth century, Christian voices were raised in protest, saying that these, too, were human souls who deserved better treatment. John Wesley's last letter was written to William Wilberforce, a member of the English Parliament, urging him to fight slavery to the end, describing it as "that execrable villainy, which is the scandal of religion, of England and of human nature."[12] When the members of the United States Congress adopted the Declaration of Independence in 1776, they stated a principle founded on Christian teaching but expressed in Enlightenment terminology about human rights: "We hold these truths to be self-evident, that all men are created equal." The deep philosophical contradiction between such a bold, biblically based statement and the practice of slavery and its later aftermath in segregation and discrimination would plague America for centuries.

In addition to human rights, we are committed to diversity. God clearly did not intend for all human beings to be the same. We are not identical clones. Instead, there are different races, languages, customs, and other human characteristics. Yet, we believe that all of us are created in the image of God. This commitment to diversity and the inclusiveness of God's purpose is expressed throughout Scripture. Philippians 2 says that "at the

40

name of Jesus every knee should bend, in heaven and on earth and under the earth, and every tongue should confess that Jesus Christ is Lord, to the glory of God the Father" (Philippians 2:10-11 NRSV). This passage has been a powerful force impelling Christians to missionary activity throughout the world, fulfilling Jesus' command to be his "witnesses in Jerusalem, in all Judea and Samaria, and to the end of the earth" (Acts 1:8).

Christians also have a strong commitment to environmental justice. Psalm 24:1-2 says, "The earth is the LORD's and everything in it, the world and its inhabitants too. Because God is the one who established it on the seas; God set it firmly on the waters." We express this commitment as a kind of stewardship. Stewards do not own the property they care for; it belongs to another. Their job is to use it in accordance with the owner's purposes and preserve it for the owner's return. For centuries, some Christians have taught that dominion meant we could use nature for our own purposes. Now that we are so numerous and so technologically powerful, the stakes have been raised. We must turn away from our past mistakes in misusing the natural world and learn to take better care of God's creation. Limiting pollution, preserving biodiversity, reducing our carbon footprint, and caring for animals are all important parts of Christian stewardship.

We Have Issues — Sin Is Real

In spite of our commitment to human rights, diversity, and environmental justice, often we don't live that way. The creation is good, and God's intentions are for us to love him and each other well, but in practice we regularly and sometimes spectacularly violate God's plan for us. We have issues. We mess things up. We are sinners.

Genesis portrays humanity as deeply flawed right from the beginning. Whether you believe that Adam and Eve were real people in the ancient past or that the story of their disobedience is a metaphorical portrayal of all humanity, their story is fundamental to Christian teaching about sin. God commanded Adam not to eat from the tree of the knowledge of good and evil. The serpent tempted Eve and she gave in, even though she knew it was wrong. Then she offered the fruit to Adam, and he did what he knew violated God's rule.

We call their actions "original sin" because it is so fundamental to human nature. All human beings are sinners. Psalm 51 expresses David's deep confession of sin after committing adultery with Bathsheba, and in verse 5 he says, "Yes, I was born in guilt, in sin, from the moment my mother conceived me."

Sin Is a Disease

Sometimes Christians talk about humanity as if sin were the whole story. It is not. Wesleyan Christians begin with the fundamental truth that we are created in God's image. Sin is like a disease that distorts that image and makes it less than what it should be.

Our belief in both human goodness and human sin is characteristic of Wesleyan teaching. We occupy the extreme center. We oppose the idea that human beings are unfailingly good and will always do the right thing if you give them a chance, but we also oppose the idea that humanity is beyond help. We recognize the serious problem of human sin, but we are optimistic about the power of God's grace.

In John Wesley's day, most Christians agreed that human beings were completely depraved. But some claimed that "completely" meant there was nothing good left in humanity at all. The Wesleyan approach was to say that "completely" meant sin had infected all parts of human nature, and there was nothing left unaffected by the disease.

If we are honest with ourselves and take seriously the commandments given in Scripture, we begin to realize just how extensive this disease is in our lives.

In the Sermon on the Mount, Jesus took several Old Testament commandments and recast them with a new and higher level of spiritual commitment. In one of these he taught:

> "You have heard that it was said, You must love your neighbor and hate your enemy. But I say to you, love your enemies and pray for those who harass you so that you will be acting as children of your Father who is in heaven. He makes the sun rise on both the evil and the good and sends rain on both the righteous and the unrighteous. If you love only those who love you, what reward do you have? Don't even the tax collectors do the same? And if you greet only your brothers and sisters, what more are you doing? Don't even the Gentiles do the same?" (Matthew 5:43-47).

Throughout the Bible there are high standards for a life of love. When we violate those standards, we are separated from God, and we cause trouble for ourselves, our families, our communities, our nation, and the world.

We can make a long list of sins that destroy the quality of human life. War and the violence of governments have taken a huge toll during the last hundred years. Two world wars involved most nations of the world and killed millions of people. Since then, regional conflicts have been very costly. Some governments have engaged in genocide against their own people, notably in Cambodia, Rwanda, and the former Yugoslavia. Harsh policies in Russia and China led to the deaths of millions by government action.

> Throughout the Bible there are high standards for a life of love.

Poverty and wealth disparity continue to destroy the quality of human life. Millions of people suffer from malnutrition, while those in other parts of the world indulge in conspicuous and wasteful consumption. Far too many people still suffer from preventable diseases such as malaria. Drug abuse, theft, murder, rape, racism, sexism, pornography, and sexual immorality are common in all parts of the world. When Wesleyans talk about human sin, there is no shortage of examples.

I once taught an adult Sunday school class without having prepared a lesson. It was my final session with that class before I took an appointment as a full-time pastor of a local church. The class was composed of mature adults who were white and upper-middle class. I started my lesson by noting that I would have to prepare sermons every week for the next several years, and I asked, "What should I preach about?" They replied, "Sin." When I asked what sins I should talk about, they named murder, theft, and other similar major crimes. I looked at the people in the room and realized that no one in the group was likely to have done any of those things. So I spent the rest of the lesson talking about racism, sexism, greed, ignoring the poor, adultery, speeding, and other sins that many of us can relate to.

When we take sin as seriously as the Bible does, we gain a greater humility. We acknowledge that we are flawed and have broken God's laws. Paul writes:

> So every single one of you who judge others is without any excuse. You condemn yourself when you judge another person because the one who is judging is doing the same things. We know that God's judgment agrees with the truth, and his judgment is against those who do these kinds of things. If you judge those who do these kinds of things while you do the same things yourself, think about this: Do you believe that you will escape God's judgment? (Romans 2:1-3)

Jesus tried to cultivate this attitude of humility in those he taught. Though Jesus had a lot in common with the Pharisees, he often used them as examples of self-righteous people who did not know their own need for God. He told this story:

> "Two people went up to the temple to pray. One was a Pharisee and the other a tax collector. The Pharisee stood and prayed about himself with these words, 'God I thank you that I'm not like everyone else—crooks, evildoers, adulterers—or even like this tax collector. I fast twice a week. I give a tenth of everything I receive. But the tax collector stood at a distance. He wouldn't even lift his eyes to look toward heaven. Rather, he struck his chest and said, 'God, show mercy to me, a sinner.' I tell you, this person went

down to his home justified rather than the Pharisee. All who lift themselves up will be brought low, and those who make themselves low will be lifted up." (Luke 18:10-14)

In our sinful ways, we human beings seek to justify ourselves. Following Jesus means focusing on our own sins first and being realistic about the ways in which sin has infected our thoughts, words, and deeds.

Salvation Is the Cure

If all human beings are sinners, what is to be done? How can we cure the disease of sin?

Wesleyans teach that God is in the business of saving sinners. God's grace has the power to end our disobedience and to shape our hearts to live according to God's purposes for us. However, God does not force us into a cure. Grace is offered to all and is available if we will accept the gift and use it. John Wesley said:

> No man living is entirely destitute of what is vulgarly called "natural conscience." But this is not natural; it is more properly termed "preventing grace." Every man has a greater or less measure of this. . . . So that no man sins because he has not grace, but because he does not use the grace which he hath. He sins because he does not use the grace which he hath.[13]

God's grace is actively helping all of us to address the problem of sin in our lives. For some people, addressing sin means learning that God loves them regardless of what they have done. For others, it means becoming aware of sin in their lives and the need to deal with it.

I remember the day when I realized I had an anger problem. I had learned from my father how to handle anger, bottling it up inside myself, refusing to express my feelings from one irritating event to the next. Finally, something would trigger my anger and I would explode. That day, my daughter had done something wrong and needed to be corrected. Instead of a measured and appropriate reproof, my response was to yell at her for almost a minute. I saw her jump and step back, with fear written on her face. I realized then that I was out of line.

I went to my Emmaus reunion group and confessed my disobedience to Christ. I told the group it was not just this one occurrence; I had an anger problem. Several of them admitted to the same issue. We then prayed for God to cure us of this sin and to change our hearts. Over time, God's grace has led me to a much better place. Paul teaches that two fruits of the Spirit are patience and kindness, and I am much more patient and kind now than I was back then. But God is still working on me!

The Wesleyan Way is a journey in which God's grace works on us to overcome the power of sin in our lives and to become the people God intended from the beginning.

The Church Is a Countercultural Community

The church of Jesus Christ is full of sinners. Far too often it lives not by the presence of Christ but out of its sinful nature. One of the remarkable qualities of the letters found in the New Testament is their honest picture, warts and all, of the early church. The community at Corinth was divided along several different lines. One division focused on the person who had baptized different members of the church. In another division, some in the community looked down on others as not having the proper spiritual gifts. There also was a division between rich and poor. But Corinth was not the only New Testament community that had problems. Later, the Book of Revelation has letters to seven churches, each of which had its shortcomings. It seems that having the church fall short of its calling is not a new thing.

It's helpful to remember, though, that at its best, the church offers a countercultural glimpse of heaven. It can be and is a means of grace, with God's grace so clearly present that the disease of sin is healed in all its manifestations.

In a world of tribalism, where people may not be invited to join a group, the church proclaims that all are welcome. In a world where racism is normal, the church teaches that Christ died for all and that God loves everyone. At our best, congregations and denominations have multiple races, nationalities, language groups, and social classes. At our best, we embody the diversity of humanity.

The Wesleyan movement has spread to most of the countries of the world. Wesleyans speak French, Russian, Swahili, Tagalog, Spanish, Vietnamese, and German as well as English and many other languages. We are a diverse group that shares a common approach to Christian beliefs and mission.

Yet, we have not lived fully into this global diversity. Tensions threaten our unity, nationally and globally. One Wesleyan church adopted a covenant that describes our aspirations for both unity and diversity:

> In covenant with God and with each other:
> We affirm our unity in Christ, and take faithful steps to live more fully into what it means to be a worldwide church in mission for the transformation of the world.
> We commit ourselves to crossing boundaries of language, culture, and social or economic status. We commit ourselves to be in ministry with all people, as we, in faithfulness to the gospel, seek to grow in mutual love and trust.

We participate in God's mission as partners in ministry, recognizing that our God-given gifts, experiences, and resources are of equal value, whether spiritual, financial, or missional.

We commit ourselves to full equity and accountability in our relationships, structures, and responsibilities for the denomination.

We enter afresh into a relationship of mutuality, creating a new sense of community and joyously living out our worldwide connection in mission for the transformation of the world.[14]

We are also countercultural in proclaiming the inherent worth of every individual. In all human societies, people form hierarchies assigning relative worth. All too often, individuals are evaluated by how they rate on scales of power, wealth, beauty, education, race, or nationality. Such discrimination makes it harder for people to reach their God-given potential. When the church is at its best, Christians tell people the gospel message:

- No matter how beautiful or handsome you are, God loves you.
- No matter how much money you have, you can accomplish great things for God by contributing what you do have.
- No matter what race or culture you were born into, the human family can be enriched by the contributions you make.
- No matter how much or how little education you have, your ideas and passion for helping others can make a difference.

When the church fully and finally embodies God's plan for a multicultural, multinational, multiracial, multilingual human family, we can embrace all the gifts and possibilities God intends for us. This means recognizing the goals God has set for the church and how far we have fallen short of them. But there is good news! God's grace is always present, inviting us to turn our lives around and move toward Christ. Repentance is a crucial step in the Wesleyan Way of salvation.

"Depth of Mercy"

Charles Wesley experienced a strong conversion three days before his brother John's conversion experience at Aldersgate Street. Charles knew that he didn't deserve to be loved by God and that he needed to change the direction of his life. The hymn expresses his realization that sometimes repentance comes when someone who is already on the way of salvation takes a detour and needs to get back on the right track. The hymn was originally titled "After a Relapse into Sin."

TRADITIONAL

Depth of mercy! Can there be
mercy still reserved for me?
Can my God his wrath forbear,
me, the chief of sinners, spare?

I have long withstood his grace,
long provoked him to his face,
would not hearken to his calls,
grieved him by a thousand falls.

I my Master have denied,
I afresh have crucified,
oft profaned his hallowed name,
put him to an open shame.

There for me the Savior stands,
shows his wounds and spreads his hands.
God is love! I know, I feel;
Jesus weeps and loves me still.

Now incline me to repent,
let me now my sins lament,
now my foul revolt deplore,
weep, believe, and sin no more.[15]

CONTEMPORARY REPHRASING

Could it be, even with God's deep depths of mercy,
that there would be enough for me?
Could God really spare me from his anger?
Even if I am a chief among sinners?

He has shown me so much grace already,
even when I provoke him on purpose,
ignore his calls to me,
and break his heart by my actions or inactions.

I have denied him.
I have crucified him again and again
when I cursed his holy name
and disregarded him to others.

But now my Savior stands before me
showing me his wounds and holding out his nail-scarred hands.
And now, I know God's love. I feel it.
Jesus weeps for love of me.

And now hear me as I repent
and confess my sins. Hear my story of rebellion
and then discover your own need of God.
Believe in him and stop sinning.

4.

Turn Your Life Around with Grace

All of us have issues. All of us have problems that need to be addressed. All of us are sinners.

Sin is breaking God's law. Our sins separate us from God, break apart our relationships with other people, and make the world a mess. If we accept the idea that sin is a disease, then all of us have unhealthy parts of our lives that need healing. How can we become healthy?

The good news is that God loves us and is trying to heal us. We don't deserve that love—it is a gift that flows from God's very nature as our loving creator. God's active love that seeks to shape our lives is called *grace*.

Wesleyan Christians believe that God's grace leads human beings from brokenness to maturity, from sin to perfection. That journey is the way of salvation. But God does not force us to make the journey. We are created in God's image, including free will.

In Genesis 3, God placed Adam and Eve in the garden with just a few rules and the ability to obey or disobey them. God did not create robots programmed to obedience. From the beginning, we have had the ability to accept or deny.

In the same way, God offers healing power but does not force it on us. God allows us to say no to his gift of love. His grace is resistible. Yet, when we accept that grace and allow God to shape our hearts, minds, and lives, amazing things can happen.

John Newton wrote a hymn that captures this experience.

Amazing grace! How sweet the sound
that saved a wretch like me!

> We are created
> in God's image,
> including free will.

I once was lost, but now am found;
was blind, but now I see.[16]

Newton was writing about his own experience of salvation. He had been the captain of a British ship sailing to Africa and America and back to Britain. One leg of his journey was transporting slaves to America. When he wrote the words "that saved a wretch like me," Newton was acknowledging his sin.

Prevenient Grace: The Grace That Comes Before

The journey of grace starts before we are ever aware of it. God is love, and God's love includes the whole world (John 3:16). Psalm 139 (NRSV) makes clear the omnipresence of God and his engagement with each human being: "If I take the wings of the morning and settle at the farthest limits of the sea, even there your hand shall lead me, and your right hand shall hold me fast" (vv. 9-10). The psalm also talks about God's engagement with us even before we were born: "For it was you who formed my inward parts; you knit me together in my mother's womb" (v. 13).

John Wesley firmly believed that every human being is the recipient of God's grace long before we are aware of it. The word *prevenient* is not familiar today, but it is helpful in describing God's work in our lives. In Latin, *pre* means before and *veni* means "to come," so prevenient grace is God's love coming into our lives before we are aware of it. Most Christians can point to ways in which God has been at working nudging us toward the Christian life. For some, it was the invitation of a friend. For others it was the still, small voice inside of us saying, "There is something more to life than what I've found so far." For one pastor who shared his story, it was his grandmother praying over his bed as he fell asleep at night.

People respond to these holy nudges in a variety of ways. Many ignore the nudges and continue life as it is. Others, sometimes after years of such promptings, finally decide to do something about it. They begin seeking God but often are unaware that it is God and faith in him for which they are looking. St. Augustine, the fifth-century bishop and theologian, put it this way: "Our hearts are restless till they find rest in Thee."[17]

Sometimes grace surprises us, and later we realize that God had something in mind much bigger and better than we had perceived at the time. I vividly remember the day my father received a phone call at our home in Greencastle, Indiana, from his longtime friend, May Titus. May said, "Jameson, we are looking for high-school youth who would like to serve on a Youth Service Fund Mission Team this summer. The opening we have is with an inner-city ministry in Tampa, Florida. Do you know anyone who might be interested?" My father covered the mouthpiece and turned to me as I sat on the staircase. "Son, do you want to go to Florida for the summer?"

Gods riches at Christ expense.

I would have done anything to get out of my hometown for the summer, so I immediately said yes. During that summer of 1969, I lived in government-owned and subsidized housing—the projects. I was a counselor at a camp. I took kids to the swimming pool and helped provide opportunities for them that otherwise were not available. I attended my first demonstration protesting the Vietnam War. That summer changed my life, because I saw that the church was a way of changing the world.

Four years later I was working full-time for The United Methodist Church and its national youth council, but I was not attending church and did not have faith in Christ. One day I was hitchhiking in northeastern Tennessee, and a truck driver stopped to pick up my friend and me. For the next two hours he talked with us about his faith in Christ. I don't remember his name or much of his story. I do remember he was active

Sinful and Sacred

E. Stanley Jones had a great line in one of his books. He said we don't break the Ten Commandments; we break ourselves on them. Sin is what we do to ourselves. We break ourselves on the commands of God, and it breaks God's heart to let us go.

Our sinfulness is part of the reality of who we are, but our sacredness is also part of that reality. One of the things I love about being a Wesleyan is that we believe the image of God is marred but not destroyed in sin. And so we human beings are a mixed bag of that which is beautiful and sacred and holy and that which is sinful and selfish and ugly. We are saints and sinners, and if the church is a place where people can claim that reality, they will be drawn to it like iron filings to a magnet, like moths to a flame.

My experience as a pastor has been that a lot of people come to church to hide and pretend that everything is okay. When we stop hiding, when instead of wasting our pain we follow our pain, then God can use it to heal us and heal others and heal our world.

Our faith journey is not a straight line. Grace isn't something we experience just once. Grace is what saves us, what keeps us saved, what sanctifies us. It's what grows us in Christ's likeness. And grace will ultimately transport us to our fullness of life in eternity.

Jorge Acevedo
Lead Pastor
Grace Church
Southwest Florida

From *The Wesleyan Way* DVD

in a Seventh-day Adventist church. What I remember most strongly is climbing down from the cab of his truck and thinking to myself, "I want the kind of faith that man has." I believe that experience was God's prevenient grace working on me.

That conversation started a four-year journey in which I sought a relationship with Christ. During that journey, there were other times when God's grace touched me. There were dead ends where I didn't find what I was seeking. There were times when grace came through a book given to me by a friend. God was continually seeking me out and offering me a relationship with him.

When we think about sharing our faith with others (a topic we will discuss in chapter 7 of this book), it's important to remember that, because of prevenient grace, we won't be taking Christ anywhere that Christ has not already been. Christ is always seeking a relationship with us. Christ is always pursuing us when we are far from him. Understanding that fact can give us great humility in our faith-sharing and can liberate us to ask questions in any situation about what God is doing and has already done.

Grace Is Grace Is Grace

When Wesleyans talk about God's grace, we sometimes get caught up in shades of meaning determined by how people experience grace and how it changes their lives. *Prevenient* grace works in us before we are even aware of it. *Convincing* grace helps us change our ways. *Justifying* grace accepts us as part of God's family. *Sanctifying* grace changes our hearts, minds, and behaviors to be more holy. When we focus on such distinctions, we sometimes make the mistake of imagining that these types of grace are four separate things.

It's not so. Grace is grace is grace. There is just one grace of God. There is just one love of God caring for us and offering us salvation. Grace is that gift we do not deserve, offered without price because of who God is and what Christ has done for us.

Think about people who love you and what they do for you. You might be able to list their behaviors in categories that would help you distinguish ways in which they care for you and have affected your life. Yet, the overwhelming reality is simply that they love you and have given you what you needed when the time was right.

God's love is the same way. When I was clueless about what I needed, God helped me understand what was missing. When I was ready to search, God gave me a glimpse of what I might do someday. At each stage of the journey, God was inviting me to take the next step, and yet God's invitation always met me where I was at the time.

God never stops loving us, and God's grace continues to work in our lives. Thus, even though I have been a Christian for several decades now, I still am growing in my faith, my hope, and my love for God and neighbor. God's grace is still actively helping me become a better disciple of Jesus Christ.

Grace Is Resistible

Grace is best understood as invitation. It is not coercive. God does not force anyone into the way of discipleship. In fact, the invitation is to love God "with all your heart, with all your being and with all your mind" (Matthew 22:37). Love requires that we freely choose to give ourselves to another.

A crucial part of the Wesleyan Way is the conviction that all aspects of God's grace are resistible. God created human beings in God's own image with the capacity to love each other and to love God. That requires the freedom either to love or to withhold love. Thus, God's grace can be resisted. God's offer of salvation can be refused. Despite God's best offers and best invitations, human beings can say no. God weeps when human beings reject his offer of salvation, but God loves us enough to let any one of us say no.

In their thinking about God, some Christians have put the greatest emphasis on God's power and control of the universe and all its creatures. Wesleyans do believe that God is sovereign and is ultimately in charge. We know that if God wills something, then he can make it happen to fulfill his plan. Some Christians, based on a few Bible passages that point in this direction, believe that God decided from the beginning of time which human beings should be saved and which should be excluded. They believe God worked out their destiny ahead of time, and that some were predestined to salvation and others were predestined to damnation. In this view, grace is irresistible: if God chooses to give you grace, you have no choice but to say yes.

Those who follow the Wesleyan Way believe that God offers everyone grace and the genuine opportunity for salvation. God's sovereign power was exercised in offering salvation to every human being. This doctrine, called universal redemption, rests on the idea that Christ died for the whole world and that every person has the opportunity for salvation. Charles Wesley expressed it this way in "Come, Sinners, to the Gospel Feast":

> Come, sinners, to the gospel feast;
> Let every soul be Jesus' guest.
> Ye need not one be left behind,
> For God hath bid all humankind.[18]

By emphasizing love as God's most important attribute, we believe God has freely chosen to limit his own power so that human beings might freely love him back or reject him.

Grace is a gift offered to each individual by God. Imagine Christ moving toward us, stretching out his arms to embrace us. Then Christ stops and waits for us to move into the embrace. The invitation is clear. Christ has made the first steps toward us. Yet, no one is forced into the embrace. Only when we step forward and accept the offered relationship does it happen.

God loves us enough to allow us to reject his love. Part of the mystery of humanity is why people choose darkness over light, hatred over love, sin over holiness, and separation from God over salvation. But they do.

Convincing Grace

In stanza 2 of "Amazing Grace," John Newton states it clearly: "'Twas grace that taught my heart to fear." One of the most important ways God loves us is to convince us that we need him.

If sin is a disease that disfigures the image of God in us, then convincing grace is the diagnosis that tells us what is wrong. All human beings are sinners, and all of us have issues that need to be addressed. Part of our sin is that we are very good at ignoring our problems and making excuses for our shortcomings. Convincing grace gives us a clear description of what our issues are when measured against God's expectations of us.

The problem is that sometimes people aren't sure what is wrong. They may have a vague sense that life is less than it should be, or they may be experiencing a crisis in which everything they value is being destroyed or going away. The medical analogy is very helpful here. Imagine you are feeling bad in a vague sort of way. There is some minor pain, but it is persistent. Slowly over time it grows, and eventually you realize it is getting in the way of your ability to function. Yet, you are not sure what is wrong. So you go to a doctor and describe your symptoms. The doctor knows what a healthy body looks like. Her examination of you includes measurements as well as listening to your experiences. If one of your organs is enlarged, or part of your body is inflamed, or some passageway is obstructed, she can tell you what the problem is. In many cases there is a way of curing the problem and the doctor can tell you what to do to regain your health. Our relationship to God is about finding the cure for our souls. We are sick, and we can move toward health by hearing God's diagnosis of what is wrong. Only then can a cure be prescribed. Convincing grace holds up the picture of what life is intended to be, and we can then see where we have fallen short.

God's Law

In Scripture, God has set the standard for our spiritual health by giving us commandments that describe the ideal way to live. These are given in the first five books of the

Bible, which Jews call "the law." Wesleyans divide God's laws into two broad categories: ceremonial laws and moral laws.

God gave ceremonial laws to the people of Israel long before the time of Christ. Many times people read Leviticus, Numbers, and other parts of the Old Testament and see that some of these ceremonial laws no longer make sense. One of the most important in the Jewish world of the first century was the law of circumcision, which applied to all male Jewish children. Leviticus 12:3 says of a male child, "On the eighth day the flesh of the boy's foreskin must be circumcised." There were also dietary laws saying that some foods, such as pork and shellfish, were not to be consumed.

As the early Christian movement preached the gospel to Gentiles—that is, people who were not Jews—a question arose. Some Gentiles came to believe in Jesus as Lord and Savior, and they received the Holy Spirit. They were baptized. But were they allowed to become Christians? Did they need to become practicing Jews before they could be Christians? Would Christianity remain a subgroup within Judaism? The question, in other words, was whether all the laws of the Old Testament, including ceremonial laws, applied to the new Gentile converts.

Peter received a revelation from God that is described in Acts 10. Afterward, Peter heard the testimony of Cornelius, a Roman centurion, about his experience of the Holy Spirit. Peter became convinced that Gentiles, too, could be part of the Christian community. In Acts 15, the leaders of the Christian community gathered in a council to discern what God intended in this new development. Since that time, Christians have taught that the moral laws of the Old Testament are still binding on all Christians, but that the ceremonial and civil laws have been left behind. In addition, the New Testament has clarified some of the Old Testament commandments and added new ones about how to live the Christian life. Together, these are called the moral law.

The moral law functions in three important ways for Christians. First, it convinces us of our sin. For example, when Christ says, "Love your enemies and pray for those who harass you" (Matthew 5:44), we understand that the hatred we may hold in our hearts for those who have wronged us is a sin. Second, the moral law helps us make the transition from a life of sin to a life of following Jesus. Third, the moral law then serves as a guide for all the rest of our lives as Christians. Even after we enter into the way of discipleship, we still struggle with the sinful parts of our lives, and the moral law provides guidance about what is right and wrong.

Wesleyans see the moral law and the gospel as two sides of the same coin. Thinking of the moral law, I'm reminded of an anecdote of two teenagers. One was frustrated and jealous because he had rules about what time to be home and what activities to engage in, while his friend had no such boundaries. Hearing the complaints of these rules, the friend, with amazing insight for an adolescent, replied, "I wish my parents loved me

The moral law provides guidance about what is right and wrong.

enough to make me follow rules." God loves us so much that God gives us the rules we should follow to live happy and fulfilled lives.

Justifying Grace

The next step to which God's grace leads us is justification. It occurs at the point in our Christian journey where we accept a new identity for ourselves, becoming disciples of Jesus. If the way of salvation is like a house, then convincing grace is the porch, where we consider going in, and justifying grace is the doorway through which we enter.

It's the place where we answer the question, "Who am I?" For each of us, the answer is best given by describing our relationships. I am Jameson and Bonnie's son, Mary Lou's husband, the father of Jameson, Marynell, and Arthur. But there is a deeper and more important way of answering the question.

This question of identity is at the heart of all religions, and each offers a different answer. Christianity teaches that God is the creator of all human beings, and this loving God has issued an invitation for each person to become one of his children. We do that by accepting Jesus as our Lord and Savior and following his way of salvation. In doing so, we promise to leave our old lives behind and begin a new life in Christ.

It's crucial to understand that we do nothing to earn this gift of a new life; God offers it to us by grace. Ephesians 2:8-9 NRSV puts it clearly: "For by grace you have been saved through faith, and this is not your own doing; it is the gift of God—not the result of works, so that no one may boast." We do nothing to earn this new identity. All we do is accept it.

Our acceptance is called faith. Faith is sometimes translated from the Greek as belief, as in John 3:16: "God so loved the world that he gave his only Son, so that everyone who believes in him won't perish but will have eternal life." Here "belief" is simply the verbal form of the word "faith".

Faith involves an intellectual component. After all, it's hard to have faith in a God who you believe does not exist. But faith is much more than that. John Wesley said that faith includes accepting what God has revealed in Scripture.

Faith also involves trust. It means relying on God, acknowledging that we are God's creatures and that God is the one on whom we rely. Many metaphors in Scripture are used to describe who God is to us. Jesus called God by the name Father, and we most often refer to God with that name. But Scripture also refers to God as creator, king, mother, lord, and redeemer. When we have faith in God, we are establishing our dependence upon him.

Wesleyans also talk about faith, in addition to belief and trust, as involving a kind of spiritual sense. Hebrews 11:1 says, "Now faith is the assurance of things hoped for, the conviction of things not seen" (NRSV). It's as if we see the world from a different perspective than we did before we came to faith. We see other people in a new light, and we perceive the whole creation in terms of God's creative purpose for it.

When we are justified, we are converted. For many people, conversion is a decisive and powerful moment, when they can say that they came to faith and finally believed. John Wesley described his conversion this way: "My heart was strangely warmed." Charles Wesley's hymn says, "My chains fell off, my heart was free, I rose, went forth, and followed Thee."[19] Many Christians have described this experience as being born again and can name a definite time and place where it happened.

My experience was that it took me more than four years after my visit with the truck driver. All that time I was seeking a powerful, instantaneous experience of conversion, and it never came. Finally it dawned on my one evening during prayer time that sometime in the previous years I had become a Christian. It was a path, not a moment. I was on the way of salvation.

The Church with Open Hearts, Minds, and Doors

The New Testament makes it clear that God seeks to save every human being. Christ died for the sins of the whole world, and God is offering his grace to everyone. Wesleyans believe in universal grace. So if God loves everyone, whom should Christians love? Wesleyans believe we should love everyone God loves, which means all people.

So, if you know someone who is not a disciple of Jesus, what should you do? I am convinced that loving someone means offering to share with him or her what you have in order to meet his or her needs. We believe that everyone needs the Lord. But how are people going to find a saving relationship with Christ unless someone introduces them?

I believe that all Christians are called to share their faith with all non-Christian people they know. We share our faith with them because we love them. This is Wesleyan evangelism, to let people know about the good news we have found.

Robert Schnase, in his book *Five Practices of Fruitful Congregations* (Nashville: Abingdon Press, 2007), has emphasized that Christians are to engage in radical hospitality. Evangelism is intended to be hospitable. The radical part means that we take the joy we have found in Christ and share it with others.

Thus the church, as the community of people who have found the way of salvation, becomes a means of God's grace and should be the place where people experience that grace most fully. We need to have open hearts so that we can love people we have not yet met. We need to have open minds so that we can engage in conversation with them and learn about their questions and struggles. We need to have open doors so that others can come in and find the faith, hope, and love that God is offering to everyone.

God in his wisdom has chosen to form a church as his primary instrument of saving the world. Our mission is to be used by God in the disciple-making process so that the world might be transformed. Part of the mechanism for that transformation is telling people about the relationship God is offering us. No matter what problems a person has, no matter what sins have been committed, no matter how far from God that person has strayed, it is possible to turn one's life around and become a disciple of Jesus.

"And Can It Be that I Should Gain"

Charles Wesley's story of his own conversion is expressed in the powerful words of this hymn.

TRADITIONAL

CONTEMPORARY REPHRASING

And can it be that I should gain
An interest in the Savior's blood!
Died he for me? who caused His pain!
For me? who him to death pursued?
Amazing love! How can it be,
That thou, my God, shouldst die for me?

I can't believe it! Could I be drawn to the God
who saved me through the power of the cross?
For me. He died for me! And I'm the one who caused his pain.
It was my sin that caused his death.
How can this be?
How could my God die for me?

'Tis mystery all: th'Immortal dies:
Who can explore his strange design?
In vain the firstborn seraph tries
To sound the depths of love divine.
'Tis mercy all! Let earth adore,
Let angel minds inquire no more.

It's a complete mystery to me: How can the Immortal God die?
What mind can understand this strange plan?
Even the very first angel, the highest in rank,
cannot convey the fullness of God's great love to us.
It's all mercy! The earth adores this Great God.
The angels need not try to get our attention anymore; Jesus has come
     and shown us God's love.

He left his Father's throne above
(So free, so infinite his grace),
Emptied himself of all but love,
And bled for Adam's helpless race:
'Tis mercy all, immense and free,
For O my God, it found out me!

Jesus left heaven
in all his freedom and his grace.
He left behind the royalty of heaven
and brought with him only love to rescue us.
And this is mercy, great and free,
and thanks be to God, this mercy reached me!

Long my imprisoned spirit lay,
Fast bound in sin and nature's night;
Thine eye diffused a quickening ray;
I woke, the dungeon flamed with light;
My chains fell off, my heart was free,
I rose, went forth, and followed Thee.

I was chained up
in sin and darkness with no way out.
But you saw me and with one look
you lit up the darkness;
the chains that held me in my sin broke loose.
I was free, really free! I got right up and followed you!

No condemnation now I dread;
Jesus, and all in him, is mine;
Alive in him, my living Head,
And clothed in righteousness divine,
Bold I approach th'eternal throne,
And claim the crown, through Christ my own.[20]

I'm not afraid of anything anymore.
I belong to Jesus and he lives in me.
I'm alive in him and he leads the way.
I am right with God
and come before him with boldness
to claim the crown that Christ saved just for me.

5.

You Are Not Alone

Years ago I participated in a leadership development group that went on a high-ropes course. The scariest exercise was climbing a thirty-foot telephone pole. We were asked to climb to the top, stand on the pole, and then jump to grab a trapeze bar about four feet away. I did it and survived with no injuries. But why would I make such an attempt? This activity appears to be foolish, crazy, and stupid.

I climbed the pole for three reasons. First, the leaders of my group expected us all to do it. I tend to be loyal to those who are leading me. Second, one of the women in my group went first and successfully completed the task. My young male ego was not about to be shown up by a woman. Third (and most important), everyone who made the jump wore a harness attached to a rope being tended by two very strong men on the ground. If I missed the trapeze, I would gently and safely be lowered to the ground.

The way of salvation described in the previous chapters is scary. If you take it seriously, it can appear to be overwhelming. When we become aware of the depth of our problems, we often give up and say we simply cannot change and so we should not bother trying.

Sometimes the problems are intellectual. Along with Jesus' disciple Thomas, we have lots of questions and want answers. Was Jesus really resurrected? How can this be?

Sometimes the problems are behavioral. When people are addicted to alcohol, drugs, or sex and enter a twelve-step program, they begin with an acknowledgement that they are in some ways powerless over their addiction.

Sometimes the problems are attitudinal. If we have been raised in a racist or sexist community, how can we genuinely come to see women or persons of color as fully human and of equal value with others?

> The way of salvation described in the previous chapters is scary.

Following Jesus appears to be really hard. God expects a lot. If we fully understand God's expectations that we love him with all of our heart, mind, soul, and strength and love our neighbors as ourselves, and that discipleship means sacrifice in order to do it, why would anyone even try? Jesus taught, "If any want to become my followers, let them deny themselves and take up their cross daily and follow me. For those who want to save their life will lose it and those who lose their life for my sake will save it (Luke 9:23-24 NRSV).

Why would anyone take up the cross? Why would anyone choose to follow Jesus? Why would anyone become a disciple?

The answer is grace. We are not alone. We don't have to make the journey by ourselves. God goes with us. We have partners on the journey.

The first partner is God, in the person of the Holy Spirit. The Spirit is God present with us all the time, giving us the grace we need to do what God has called us to do. Grace is like the harness I wore on the telephone pole. The Holy Spirit keeps us safe. In one of the worship statements used many years ago, the congregation repeated an important affirmation of faith: "In life, in death, in life beyond death, we are not alone. Thanks be to God!" There is a great sense of mystery in this statement. God is all-powerful and could force us to be whatever he intends. But God is love, and he wills that we love him back and freely choose to follow the way of salvation.

There are other partners on the journey. When I jumped off the pole, I was following what others had done. My group was cheering me on, letting me know they had confidence that I could do it. The church of Jesus Christ is like that. We are not the first generation of Christians, and I expect we will not be the last. All those who have gone before us form what the book of Hebrews calls "a great cloud of witnesses." I envision this cloud of witnesses to be like people lining the sidewalks of a marathon race. They have already finished the race and are urging us on as we "run the race laid out in front of us" (Hebrews 12:1-2).

The Holy Spirit and the Means of Grace

New Christians and others exploring the way of salvation might ask a practical question: "If God really is trying to save us, how do we get in touch with this grace you're talking about? How does the presence of the Holy Spirit really make a difference?"

John Wesley asked the same question. He knew that God is love and is actively trying to save people. He also knew that God has commanded certain practices for people to follow, and he believed that these commandments were given by God for our salvation. They were practices that conveyed God's grace to us.

It's important to note that Wesley, like most other Christians, believed that God offers grace in a wide variety of ways. For example, people connect with God through the beauty of creation, and sometimes God gives these people and others a special revelation outside the normal channels.

But it's also important to acknowledge the normal channels. These means of grace are the ways in which God has promised to be present with human beings and to connect with them.

The church itself is a means of grace. Jesus told the leader of the disciples, "I tell you that you are Peter. And I'll build my church on this rock. The gates of the underworld won't be able to stand against it" (Matthew 16:18). Jesus promised, "For where two or three are gathered in my name, I am there with them" (Matthew 18:20). He promised

---

Christ Himself

When Jesus talks about losing your life, it can take on a lot of different forms. For some of us, it just means letting go of the past. For some people, it means forgiving themselves. For some people, it means letting go of an addiction. For others, it means letting go of patterns that are destructive. What it really means is going toward something as much as letting go of something. Denying myself, yes, but not with the focus on what I'm losing but what I'm gaining in Christ.

When invited, God comes. When invited, the Holy Spirit comes. Jesus is clear about this when he says I will pray and the Father will send you a comforter. The Father will send you a helper, and that is the Holy Spirit.

When we look at baptism, when we look at Holy Communion, being a part of a church, being in worship, being in a small group, it's not a small group that changes your life. It's not the servant. It's not the preacher. It's actually Christ himself.

Once you've said yes to Christ as your constant companion, it is such a joy to have Christ with you in great times but also in difficult times. I've seen hundreds of church members come from places of fear, places of addiction, places of lost-ness, and when they accept Christ they are different. They have changed, and their lives are never the same.

It doesn't mean life will be easy. It doesn't mean you'll escape the bad things. But the joy we have as Christians is that Christ is our companion. You are not alone. He will go through it with you.

Jessica Moffatt Seay
Senior Pastor
First United Methodist Church
Ardmore, Oklahoma

From *The Wesleyan Way* DVD

---

before his death that after he was gone, God would send another comforter to take his place and would not leave the disciples orphaned. Acts 2 describes the powerful presence of that comforter, the Holy Spirit, present at Pentecost some fifty days after Christ's resurrection, on what has been described as the church's birthday.

Among the means of grace provided by the church are the holy practices that God has commanded us to use. Five of these are commandments: baptism, Holy Communion, Scripture, prayer, and worship. While all of these are means of grace, the first two are sacraments because of the special significance they play in the Christian life. But all five are ways in which Christians stay in love with God.

For Wesleyans, there are two sacraments. Roman Catholics and others count more, but Wesleyan Christians, along with other Protestants, recognize only Holy Communion and baptism. These sacraments are outward and visible signs of an inward and spiritual grace offered by God. God is not limited to sacraments in his work, but they are reliable means by which God has promised to connect with those who faithfully partake of them.

Baptism and Conversion

Baptism is the sacrament whereby God washes away our sin and accepts us into the family of God. Water is the symbolic means of showing that we have been cleansed and forgiven of our separation from God. With it, we are marked as disciples and become Christians. Wesleyans believe that in baptism, God touches our lives in a special way. Once we are baptized, we become members of Christ's body, the church.

Ever since the sixteenth century, Christians have disagreed about who can be baptized and how much water should be used. From the very early days of the Christian movement (no one is quite sure how early, but at least in the second century), infants were baptized by the church. Since we believe all human beings are sinners, infants need cleansing, too. More important, Jesus had a special regard for children and said, "Allow the children to come to me . . . Don't forbid them, because the kingdom of heaven belongs to people like these children" (Matthew 19:14). In keeping with the earliest Christian traditions, Wesleyan Christians baptize their babies.

When infants are baptized, the whole congregation promises to help the Christian parents raise them in the faith. The youngsters need to be taught to read the Bible, worship, and receive the sacrament of Holy Communion. In other words, they should participate in the means of grace through the life of the church. Later the church offers a series of classes and activities, called confirmation, to deepen their understanding of the faith. At the end of it, young people decide whether they want to accept the grace offered at baptism and to make a personal commitment to Christ, becoming professing or full members of the church.

A person can be baptized at any age. In many churches, the confirmation class will include young people who have never been baptized. For them the decision to follow Jesus as a disciple will then include the sacrament of baptism.

There are also people who come to faith as adults. They may have been converted in a revival meeting, in a Bible study group, or through conversation with friends. They have decided to leave a sinful life behind and turn to God. Accepting Jesus Christ as Lord and Savior is the first step, and baptism is God's way of marking them sacramentally.

Wesleyans believe that a small amount of water is sufficient for baptism. There is nothing wrong with immersing a person completely under the water, as some churches do in baptism, and sometimes the person chooses that method. But baptism by sprinkling is a valid form of the sacrament.

> Accepting Jesus Christ as Lord and Savior is the first step.

Though there are many possible paths into Christian discipleship, one more deserves mention. Someone born into a Christian family might be baptized as an infant and even confirmed to become a professing member of the church. As their life progresses, however, they might drop out of church and even deny that Christ is Lord. They have left the way of salvation and pursued other paths and perhaps other religions as well. What happens if this person comes back to follow Jesus?

Wesleyans teach that we can be baptized only once. When we are marked as part of God's family, he is faithful to the grace given in the sacrament. God doesn't change. However we wander, if we come back and reaffirm our relationship to Christ, we will be accepted just as if we had not left. No re-baptism is necessary or even allowed. Wesleyans do have a ceremony of remembering and reaffirming our baptism, because that is something all Christians can profit from.

What happens if someone changes denominations? Wesleyans believe that baptism initiates the believer into the church, the body of Christ. Because we recognize other denominations as fellow Christians, we recognize the validity of their baptism. Thus, Wesleyans do not re-baptize those who were baptized in other denominations. Three things are necessary for valid baptism: the proper intention, the use of water, and the triune name of God as Father, Son, and Holy Spirit.

Holy Communion

The repeatable sacrament is Holy Communion. Christ commanded his disciples during the last supper he had before his crucifixion. That supper is the Passover meal that Jews eat every year to commemorate God's action in saving them from slavery in Egypt. Families traditionally eat it together, and Jesus ate it with his disciples.

Jesus transformed the Passover supper into a remembrance of his sacrifice for all humanity. Luke 22:19-20 recounts the crucial action in these words:

> After taking the bread and giving thanks, he broke it and gave it to them, saying, "This is my body, which is given for you. Do this in remembrance of me." In the same way, he took the cup after the meal and said, "This cup is the new covenant by my blood, which is poured out for you."

Three days later, on the first Easter afternoon, the resurrected Jesus appeared to Cleopas and a friend as they walked to Emmaus. Jesus explained why the Messiah had to die, but they did not recognize him. It was in the breaking of bread in Emmaus that Christ was revealed to these early disciples.

For generations of Christians, the sacrament of the Lord's Supper has been a powerful means of grace. In many churches this meal is called the Eucharist, because that word in Greek means "thank you." In Wesleyan practice, the pastor consecrates the elements by offering a prayer of thanksgiving to God for all that God has done. Such prayers are Trinitarian, starting by thanking God the Father, then recounting what God the Son did in the Last Supper, and then asking for the presence of the Holy Spirit in the elements that are about to be consumed.

Christ has promised to be truly present in the meal.

For many Wesleyans, our tradition of having circuit-riding pastors meant that Communion was celebrated only once a month. Long after the circuit riders dismounted and churches had resident pastors, that pattern continued, often on the first Sunday of the month. However, more and more Wesleyans are going back to John Wesley's practice. His sermon "The Duty of Constant Communion" made the argument that God expects us to receive the sacrament as often as we possibly can, but at least on every Sunday.

Wesleyans have made one other change that was and may still be controversial. In the 1800s we became concerned about the evils that alcohol abuse was bringing to families. For the protection of families and the promotion of sober and hardworking people, we first advocated temperance in the use of alcohol. As time went on, we advocated abstinence. But how can we do that if Holy Communion requires the wine that Jesus used at the Last Supper? About that time, a Methodist layman named Welch invented a process for making unfermented wine—grape juice. Because of our commitment to minimize or avoid alcohol use, we have traditionally celebrated Communion with grape juice instead of wine.

We believe that Christ is truly present in the elements of bread and wine. We do not believe in transubstantiation, in which the bread becomes something other than bread and the juice something other than juice. At the same time, we believe the bread and wine are more than symbols. Christ has promised to be truly present in the meal. Wesleyans regard this as a mystery. Charles expressed it clearly in "O the Depth of Love Divine":

> O the depth of love divine, the unfathomable grace!
> Who shall say how bread and wine God into us conveys!
> How the bread his flesh imparts, how the wine transmits his blood,
> Fills his faithful people's hearts with all the life of God! . . .
>
> Sure and real is the grace, the manner be unknown;
> Only meet us in thy ways and perfect us in one.
> Let us taste the heavenly powers, Lord, we ask for nothing more.
> Thine to bless, 'tis only ours to wonder and adore.[21]

The bread and wine, without actually changing, become vehicles for Christ's presence in the sacred meal. Christ has promised that these "feeble elements" will convey the power of God's love into our lives. The elements are more than a symbol and less than a magically transformed metaphysical body of Christ. For us, they become the body and blood of Christ, and they change lives.

Scripture

John Wesley taught that reading the Bible is a means of God's grace. The preface to his *Sermons* includes these words:

> I want to know one thing, the way to heaven—how to land safe on that happy shore. God himself has condescended to teach the way: for this very end he came down from heaven. He hath written it down in a book. O give me that book! At any price give me the book of God! I have it. Here is knowledge enough for me. Let me be *homo unius libri*.[22]

For Wesleyans, the Bible is the basic authority for our faith and practice. It is the inspired word of God that governs how we follow Christ.

Wesleyans do not teach that Scripture is infallible. Instead, we teach that the Bible contains all things necessary to salvation. One church's "Confession of Faith" says,

> We believe the Holy Bible, Old and New Testaments, reveals the Word of God so far as it is necessary for our salvation. It is to be received through the Holy Spirit as the true rule and guide for faith and practice. Whatever is not revealed

in or established by the Holy Scriptures is not to be made an article of faith
nor is it to be taught as essential to salvation.[23]

There are parts of the Bible that are hard to understand and parts that appear to conflict with the main themes and messages of the whole Bible. Wesleyan Christians seek
to follow the whole Bible and try to resist citing just one passage in isolation from the
rest of what God has revealed in Scripture. It is the whole message of Scripture that
matters.

Wesleyans believe that the Bible has both human and divine attributes. Its human
side is revealed in how it came to be. Modern scholarship has made very important contributions in analyzing the formation of the text. The sixty-six books of the Bible were
created over centuries and from a variety of sources. The books were written in Hebrew,
Aramaic, and Greek, and they show the linguistic and cultural conditions of the varying
times in which they were first composed. We believe that God accommodated himself
to people's ability at the time to understand what God was trying to say.

At the same time, the Bible is fully divine. It is inspired. The Holy Spirit used the
authors to communicate important messages that God wanted his people to understand.
Yet, because there are so many different literary styles, and the books were composed
over so many centuries in so many different cultural contexts, the Bible is sometimes
hard to understand. Dr. Albert Outler, the twentieth-century Methodist theologian mentioned previously, put it this way: "The Bible is complex enough to challenge people
who have spent their lives studying it, and simple enough that a baby Christian can
benefit from reading it."[24]

Mark Twain is reputed to have said, "It is not the parts of the Bible I don't understand that bother me." In other words, the parts that most challenge us are the parts that
are clear. These have the capacity to connect us with God. The Bible is, in that way, a
means of grace.

God has revealed what we need to know in the Old and New Testaments, and
studying Scripture gives us what we need. Bible study is best done in a group of
people. It is complex enough that many different perspectives are helpful in properly
interpreting it.

Wesleyan Christians try to look at the entirety of Scripture. They see the main theme
of the Bible as the story of a loving God who is constantly seeking to save his creation
and help it become what he intended all along. You can see that this main theme of the
Bible is in fact the way of salvation we are studying here. Other Christians empha-
size different themes, but the Wesleyan view is that God is love and is seeking to save
humanity from its sins.

Prayer

Prayer is a means of grace. Whether one prays alone or in a congregation, silently or aloud, speaking spontaneously or reading written words, communicating with God can bring us closer to his love and his desires for our lives.

In the Bible we are commanded to pray. Sometimes Jesus assumes we are doing it and begins a commandment by saying, "When you pray…" (see Matthew 6:5-8). He also gives us what has come to be known as the Lord's Prayer (Matthew 6:9-13). In 1 Thessalonians 5:17, we are told to pray without ceasing.

There are many different types of prayer. Some prayers praise God. In these words we acknowledge that God is God and we are not God. We give him honor, praise, and glory, and we acknowledge that we are his creatures. When we worship the Lord and proclaim his nature, we come to a deeper understanding of who we are as human beings.

Other prayers confess our sins. These are opportunities for us to tell God the truth about ourselves and seek his forgiveness. Some people don't like prayers of confession. In one church I served, a person who was considering joining the church urged me not to include a prayer of confession during worship. As a young pastor I knew there was flexibility in our worship style, and I recognized that some people would feel bad about such a prayer. So I complied, and we had no prayer of confession for the next several weeks. During that time, my potential church member abandoned his wife and daughter and left town to live with his secretary. Since then, I have known that prayers of confession are spiritually helpful.

The best prayers of confession are ones in which we acknowledge our inability to solve our own problems, and we ask for God's help. We invite the Holy Spirit to guide us, give us wisdom, strengthen our weaknesses, and remove us from temptation. Sometimes we are not asking for forgiveness so much as asking for help in dealing with problems or opportunities that are beyond our capacities. Every time I preach, I pray these words: "Almighty God, we thank you for the presence of the Holy Spirit in this place, for we trust your promise that where two or three are gathered, there you will be also. But sometimes we don't get it. So we ask: Open our eyes that we might see you. Give us ears to hear your word. And then give us hands and feet that we might be doers of the word and not hearers only."

We acknowledge our inability to solve our own problems, and we ask for God's help.

Other prayers are to intercede, or request help, for others. We pray that those who are sick might be healed. We pray that those in danger might be kept safe. We pray that those who are hungry might be fed. We pray that those who grieve might be comforted. We pray that wars might end and injustice be replaced by God's kingdom on earth. We pray for our enemies.

Sometimes our prayers are answered by God's actions for others. But sometimes we hear a word from the Lord about our own behavior, our own priorities, and our own opportunities. Prayer can change both the world outside and the world inside us. Prayer is partly telling God what we need to say, but it is also listening for God's word to us.

Worship

John Wesley once said, "Christianity is essentially a social religion, and that to turn it into a solitary religion is indeed to destroy it."[25] When we become disciples of Jesus, we are baptized into his body. The members of his body gather every Lord's Day (that is, every Sunday) to worship God. The word *worship* is a shortened form of the Old English word *woerthship*, or proclaiming God's worth—that God is God and we are not. By praising the Lord, we accept our rightful place as creatures of God. Psalm 100 makes it clear: "Worship the LORD with gladness; come into his presence with singing. Know that the LORD is God. It is he that made us, and we are his; we are his people, and the sheep of his pasture" (NRSV).

It is in worship that we remind ourselves who we are and whose we are. We do that through prayer, singing, celebrating the sacraments of Communion and baptism, and reading the Bible together. An important part of worship is preaching the word. People who have been Christians for decades have heard hundreds of sermons. A good sermon is one that faithfully communicates the message of the Bible and connects it with the life circumstances of its hearers. Many times a sermon will strike listeners as being fresh and new, even if they have heard many sermons on the same text before.

Small Groups

One important characteristic of early Methodism was the class meeting. To belong to the Methodist society meant attending a class in which the members watched over one another in love and helped other class members progress in the way of salvation. Members asked each other every week, "How is it with your soul?" Members told of their spiritual struggles and how they were progressing on the way of salvation.

Over time, most Wesleyans gave up the formal accountability systems of the class meeting, but Sunday school classes have picked up some of the same functions. More recently, small groups have attempted to re-create the dynamics and accountability of the class meeting. Emmaus reunion groups take the basic experience of the Walk to Emmaus program and ask group members to share their times of being closest to Christ, their worst denial of discipleship, and their Christian action, study, and piety or prayer life. The practice of covenant discipleship invites participates to make a covenant or promise together, then hold each other accountable for what they have agreed to do. In his book *Waking to God's Dream* (Nashville: Abingdon Press, 1999), Richard Wills describes Wesleyan fellowship groups that have five functions: prayer, fellowship, study, accountability, and service. I believe that every Christian should belong to a small group that in some way serves these five purposes.

Sacrificial Service and Giving

In the parable of the sheep and the goats (Matthew 25:31-46), Jesus teaches that we are to feed the hungry, give water to the thirsty, welcome the stranger, clothe the naked, and visit those who are sick or in prison. For many years, people who have followed these commands have described the great blessings they received from doing it—in addition, of course, to the blessings bestowed on the people they helped.

One of Jesus' most difficult and yet most important teachings says, "If any want to become my followers, let them deny themselves and take up their cross daily and follow me. For those who want to save their life will lose it, and those who lose their life for my sake will save it" (Luke 9:23-24 NRSV).

We live in a culture that values material things and encourages us to accumulate them. We take care of ourselves and ignore the needs of others. The way of discipleship teaches the opposite: that by giving of our time, talent, and money, we will be blessed far beyond what we have given. For it is in giving away our life for the sake of the gospel that we truly find it.

Some people are surprised to learn that Jesus talked more about money and how to use it than he did about prayer. Christians should be cultivating the spiritual gift of extravagant generosity. Wesley, in fact, had three rules for the use of money: make all you can, save all you can, and give all you can.

Living as Disciples

How do we summarize the Christian practices we have discussed? One way is in the simple phrase "worship plus group." The Christian life is one lived by grace through faith. When we accept Christ as Lord and Savior and are baptized into his body, we set out on a journey to live as his disciples. But we need help on the journey. That help comes in the various means of grace. Weekly worship in the gathered community is crucial. There, we regularly participate in the sacrament of Holy Communion. There we pray with our fellow Christians, hear the Word of God proclaimed, praise and worship God. We are challenged to tithe our income. We hear opportunities to carry God's love into the world.

Our small groups hold us accountable for using the means of grace. Ideally, the group practices prayer, fellowship, study, accountability, and service. Members encourage each other, share insights about how to handle tough times, support each other, and keep each other on the path of discipleship. When these things happen with love, then all sorts of amazing things are possible.

"Amazing Grace"

John Newton's powerful hymn, quoted briefly before, has guided generations on the Christian journey by describing the power of grace to change our lives. We quote it in its entirety here, including a final stanza that was added later and has inspired generations of Christians to envision a hope of life eternal with the Lord.

TRADITIONAL	CONTEMPORARY REPHRASING
Amazing grace! How sweet the sound that saved a wretch like me! I once was lost, but now am found; was blind, but now I see.	God's grace is amazing. It's like the sound of a sweet song of salvation to a sinner like me. See, I was lost but God found me and put me on his path. I was blind to my need of God, but now I see it.
'Twas grace that taught my heart to fear, and grace my fears relieved; how precious did that grace appear the hour I first believed.	Grace taught me to fear God, but God's grace also dispelled all my fears. God's grace is precious to me and came to me the very moment I professed my belief in the God of grace.
Through many dangers, toils, and snares, I have already come; 'tis grace hath brought me safe thus far, and grace will lead me home.	I have been on a wild ride in life— danger, struggles, temptations. But grace got me safely to this point and grace will get me all the way to my eternal home.
The Lord has promised good to me, his word my hope secures; he will my shield and portion be, as long as life endures.	The Lord promises good things for me. I firm up my hope in his promises by knowing his word. He is my protector and everything I will ever need for my whole life.
Yea, when this flesh and heart shall fail, and mortal life shall cease, I shall possess, within the veil, a life of joy and peace.	When my body starts to fail me and my earthly life ends, I will see God in heaven and know a life of joy and peace forever.
When we've been there ten thousand years, bright shining as the sun, we've no less days to sing God's praise than when we'd first begun.[26]	And even when we've been living with God in the brilliant light of heaven for ten thousand years, we get the privilege of singing God's praises for ten thousand more!

6.

Transform Yourself and the World

The key to happiness, fulfillment, and salvation is becoming the person God intended you to be. God has a plan for your life, and that plan calls for you to grow up. No, we are not talking being old enough to vote and sign contracts. We are not talking about increasing in height or weight. And we are not talking about getting married and having children or any of the other outward trappings of adulthood.

Spiritual maturity is about your heart being transformed to become more and more like Jesus. Jesus is the model for what grown-up men and women should be like, and we want to become more like him.

The best way to describe that model is to quote Jesus himself. When asked the greatest commandment of the law, Jesus replied in Matthew 22:37-40, "You must love the Lord your God with all your heart, with all your being, and with all your mind. This is the first and greatest commandment. And the second is like it: You must love your neighbor as you love yourself. All the Law and the Prophets depend on these two commands." The goal of Christians is to love God so completely and love their neighbors as themselves so fully that everything they think, say, and do is motivated by love.

Perhaps you've known someone who exemplifies this level of maturity. For me it was Elizabeth Snell. When I became her pastor, Elizabeth was in her eighties and was busily taking care of many old people in her community. She loved the Lord with a heart as pure as anyone I have ever known. She was a prayer warrior, spending significant

> *God has a plan for your life, and that plan calls for you to grow up.*

time each day with the Lord. She read her Upper Room devotional magazine daily and spent time in Bible study. She visited her neighbors and often made trips for them to the grocery store or pharmacy. During her visits, she asked about their relationship with Christ. Often she would share her faith and invite her neighbors to become Christians as well. On one notable occasion she said to me, "Preacher, I have been visiting this neighbor, and I am just about ready for you to come and visit him. The harvest is just about ready." A few weeks after that, the man was in the hospital and asked to see me. Then and there he committed his life to Christ. His family started attending church as well. When I grow up, I want to be like Elizabeth Snell. She was not famous. She was not wealthy. She did not have a college education. But she was rich in all the things that matter most in life: faith, hope, love, and service to God and neighbor.

How does we make progress toward that kind of maturity? The first step is clarity about what God is hoping to do through you.

Transform Your Heart

The New Testament has many different ways of describing God's will for our lives. Jesus' Sermon on the Mount, found in Matthew 5–7, gives several powerful descriptions of the Christian life. He began by saying that several different groups of people are blessed: the poor in spirit, those who mourn, the meek, those who hunger and thirst for righteousness, the merciful, the pure in heart, the peacemakers, and those who are persecuted for Christ's sake. John Wesley translated the Greek word *makarios* as "happy" instead of "blessed," pointing to the Wesleyan belief that those who do God's will find fulfillment, joy, and deep happiness in this life and in the world to come.

Jesus went on to quote several Old Testament laws and raise them to a new, spiritual level. For example, he cited "Don't commit murder" and then carried it further: "Everyone who is angry with their brother or sister will be in danger of judgment. If they say to their brother or sister, 'You idiot,' they will be in danger of being condemned by the governing council. And if they say, 'You fool,' they will be in danger of fiery hell" (Matthew 5:22). He cited "Don't commit adultery" and extended it: "But I say to you that every man who looks at a woman lustfully has already committed adultery in his heart" (Matthew 5:28).

The apostle Paul interpreted Jesus' words with additional commandments. In Romans 12:9-17, Paul wrote:

> Love should be shown without pretending. Hate evil, and hold on to what
> is good. Love each other like the members of your family. Be the best at

showing honor to each other. Don't hesitate to be enthusiastic—be on fire in the Spirit as you serve the Lord! Be happy in your hope, stand your ground when you're in trouble, and devote yourselves to prayer. Contribute to the needs of God's people, and welcome strangers into your home. Bless people who harass you—bless and don't curse them. Be happy with those who are happy, and cry with those who are crying. Consider everyone as equal, and don't think that you're better than anyone else. Instead associate with people who have no status. Don't think that you're so smart. Don't pay back anyone

Jesus Joy

Church isn't about Sunday mornings. Sunday morning is the most segregated hour in the week. Everybody goes to his or her little place of comfort. They're pew potatoes. Then they go home. But God is calling us. I mean, the only thing we were ever asked to do is be a servant.

When you fall in love with Jesus, you want to serve. You want to give. You want to be outside the walls of the church, telling somebody else your story, because the most powerful thing you have is your testimony.

I grew up in a home with a single parent, and I know what it's like to run out of money at the end of the month. So I put bags of food in the trunk of my car, and I drive around and look for people—single moms, single dads, people who work hard every day making seven or eight dollars an hour. I pull up next to them, pop my trunk, hop out, and give them two bags of food. You should see the looks I get when I say, "It's not me. It's the Christ inside me." I don't want any credit. I don't want anything.

When you learn the joy in serving, when you start getting the joy, I call it Jesus Joy, then it doesn't matter if you just lost your job or not. I tell people: when you're down, go serve. When you don't feel right, go do something for somebody else, because that's what Jesus did for us. Then you'll find the peace that passes all understanding.

Felicia Hopkins
Senior Associate Pastor
St. Mark's United Methodist Church
El Paso, Texas

From *The Wesleyan Way* DVD

for their evil actions with evil actions, but show respect for what everyone
else believes is good.

These additional commandments can be seen as Paul's way of helping the early
Christians follow Jesus' model. In other passages, such 1 Corinthians 12–13, Paul
addressed specific congregational struggles and described what love meant in the midst
of their divisions.

Paul gave us a helpful summary of the Christian life in his letter to the Galatians,
in which he distinguished between the way of the flesh and life in the Spirit. The way
of the flesh includes a number of behaviors which Paul labeled as immoral: "sexual
immorality, moral corruption, doing whatever feels good, idolatry, drug use and casting
spells, hate, fighting, obsession, losing your temper, competitive opposition, conflict,
selfishness, group rivalry, jealousy, drunkenness, partying, and other things like that"
(Galatians 5:19-21). In contrast, those who have been baptized and are following Jesus
live in the power of the Holy Spirit, which is working on the believers' hearts to transform them. Qualities that Paul calls "fruit of the Spirit" include love, joy, peace, patience,
kindness, goodness, faithfulness, gentleness, and self-control (Galatians 5:22-23).

One way of reminding ourselves about God's desire to transform our lives is to
memorize these nine qualities and continually measure ourselves against them. When
my children were growing up, they could all repeat the qualities from memory. Based
on personal experience, I can report that the problem with teaching your children these
nine standards of Christian behavior is that when they grow up, they might ask you
about living them out yourself.

Transform Your Judgment

But there's more to the goal of Christian life than transforming your heart and behavior. There are the larger issues of evil and immorality in our communities and nations,
and Christians are called to address them.

The basis for this way of thinking about big issues is the boundary-crossing nature
of Jesus' ministry. Over and over, Jesus broke the socially exclusive norms of his culture to build relationships with those considered outcasts by the Jews. He spoke with
a Samaritan woman at Jacob's well (John 4:5-41). When walking through Jericho, he
spoke directly to a tax collector named Zacchaeus, then ate a meal with Zacchaeus and
led him to make restitution to those he had wronged (Luke 19:1-10). Jesus spoke with a
Roman centurion and healed his servant (Matthew 8:5-13). He healed the daughter of a
Syrophoenician woman (Mark 7:24-30). In all these circumstances, Jewish practice was
to seek righteousness by avoiding sinners and outcasts such as these people. Instead,
Jesus reached out to them, met their needs, and included them in his ministry.

Jesus' boundary-crossing ministry was the impetus for the early Christians to include Gentiles in the Christian movement. This practice was controversial for many years, and yet the Holy Spirit told the Council of Jerusalem that the Christian movement was bigger than Judaism. It was about the gospel being shared with the whole world, "to the end of the earth" (Acts 1:8).

Mission with the Poor

In the parable of the sheep and the goats mentioned previously, Jesus stressed the importance of how we treat the hungry, the thirsty, the naked, the stranger, and those in prison. He concluded, "As you did it to one of the least of these brothers and sisters of mine, , you have done it for me" (Matthew 25:40).

Jesus' parable fit very well with the Old Testament teaching that God's people (Israel) were to take special care of widows, orphans, strangers, and other poor people in their midst. The prophets were very clear about this: Isaiah, Jeremiah, Habakkuk, Amos, and Ezekiel all uttered words from the Lord similar to these from Zechariah 7:9-10: "Make just and faithful decisions; show kindness and compassion to each other! Don't oppress the widow, the orphan, the stranger, and the poor; don't plan evil against each other!"

How we Christians treat the poor is crucial. In fact, part of what converted most of the Roman Empire to Christianity was the early Christians' treatment of the poor. Too many Christians today have forgotten Jesus' commandments about taking care of those less fortunate. It's a big problem when Christians become self-centered and focused on how God will bless them rather than trying to bless others.

One of the principal Christian teachings is that when people are accepted into the body of Christ, they are blessed and become a blessing to others. We share the faith with them to save their souls, but we help their bodies as well, by feeding them, bringing them justice, and ending their oppression.

Mission *with* the poor is different from mission *to* the poor. Poverty does not rob people of their humanity; the best gift we can give them is a relationship. Often our compassion for the poor amounts to an occasional handout, rather than a long-term investment in caring, supporting, teaching, and empowering. All people, including those who are poor, have amazing resources that can be used to address their problems. Methodism began as a movement in England among poor people who learned values and skills from Wesleyan preaching and small groups that allowed them not only to grow in faith but also to make progress in life skills as well.

Social Justice

Christianity has always addressed major issues facing the cultures in which it ministered. In the 1700s, many Christians in Great Britain were starting to believe that the practice of slavery violated Christian beliefs. John Wesley's last letter was written to William Wilberforce, an evangelical member of Parliament, encouraging him to continue the fight to end slavery. The General Rules, defining practices that Methodists were to avoid, said that no one who owned slaves could belong to the Methodist movement. However, as the movement spread through the southern United States in the early 1800s, Bishop Asbury and other leaders compromised and dropped that requirement for Methodist membership.

Later in the history of the Wesleyan movement, the church began a witness for temperance, arguing that the abuse of alcohol was bad for women, children, and families. Wesleyans had long argued against the use of "spirituous liquors" and against drunkenness. As the nineteenth century progressed, Methodist witness moved from temperate use to prohibition. The same was true of the witness against gambling, which, though never condemned explicitly in Scripture, was damaging family life. Wesleyans living on the frontier saw how people would spend their earnings on gambling rather than on their children, and so the witness against this practice spread.

Christians of good character and equal commitment to Christ will have disagreements.

The early 1900s brought more sophisticated tools of analysis about social problems and opportunities. Using these, Wesleyan Christians investigated and spoke out on many questions such as war and peace, unions and economic justice, racism and the environment. One Wesleyan denomination adopted a set of social principles and resolutions in 1908. Not all Christians will agree with the social principles and resolutions of their church; the important thing is for all of us to think seriously about the big problems of our time from a Christian perspective.

During the last 150 years we have seen an amazing transformation of global wealth. As industrialization has transformed the world, people have accumulated immense quantities of material goods. Food production has increased. At the same time, the world's population has exploded, and the numbers of people living in poverty has increased dramatically. It was in 1964 that President Lyndon Johnson declared a "war on poverty," and we still are fighting it today. New diseases such as HIV/AIDS have erupted, and additional problems have arisen, notably genocides and the difficulties caused by the end of colonialism in the Middle East, Africa, Latin America, and Asia.

Christians must bring their best judgment to bear on these problems and more so that biblical values can be applied in all sectors of all societies throughout the world.

Yet, precisely because the problems are complex, Christians of good character and equal commitment to Christ will have disagreements. In some cases we won't prioritize problems in the same way; in other cases, we will address the same problems in radically different ways. I have often made the point that George W. Bush and Hilary Rodham Clinton are both active and faithful United Methodist Christians, and yet they belong to different political parties and have different understandings about applying Christian faith in the world.

Catholic Spirit

One of the hallmarks of Wesleyan Christianity has been our ability to focus on the most important things while respecting disagreements on matters of opinion. John Wesley's sermon "Catholic Spirit" should be mandatory reading for anyone with strong opinions about theological and political matters. In that sermon, Wesley says that essential truths are different from matters of opinion. Thus, differing beliefs and practices have grown up among Christians over time. In his day, the doctrine of predestination was divisive. He firmly believed that God had empowered all human beings with sufficient grace to be saved if they would only use it, whereas his friend George Whitefield, a member of the Holy Club at Oxford, was a Calvinistic Methodist who believed that such choices were predestined. Wesley knew there were strong scriptural arguments in favor of predestination, but he could not reconcile the doctrine with the overall message of a loving God who died for the sins of the whole world.

Wesley's view of Catholic Spirit included the idea that on matters of opinion, it is important to realize that one's own view might be wrong. He urged people to think carefully about important issues, because it does matter what you think and how you respond. But if you know there is a chance—however small—that you might be wrong, then you must approach those who disagree in a more charitable spirit.

Wesley described Catholic Spirit as universal love. His sermon is based on 2 Kings 10:15, focusing on the verse from the King James Version, "Is thine heart right, as my heart is with thy heart? If it be, give me thine hand."

> But although a difference in opinions or modes of worship may prevent an entire external union, yet need it prevent our union in affection? Though we cannot think alike, may we not love alike? May we not be of one heart, though we are not of one opinion? Without all doubt, we may. Herein all the children of God may unite, notwithstanding these smaller differences. These remaining as they are, they may forward one another in love and in good works.[27]

At various times in history, communities have been torn apart by rivalries, partisan violence, deliberate misunderstandings, and deep divisions. Sometimes those divisions have had religious overtones, pitting Protestants against Catholics, Jews against Christians, Christians against Muslims. Within denominations and congregations, internal conflicts have often caused similar conflicts. In all such instances, a commitment to Catholic Spirit is an important key to the unity of a nation or a people, and to the body of Christ.

Sanctification by Grace

Sometimes the goal of living a holy life dedicated to God seems unreachable. When I read Scripture, I glimpse God's will for my life, and I begin to think, "Oh, God, I cannot do this." It's especially true when I read Matthew 5:48, in which Jesus said, "Be perfect, therefore, as your heavenly Father is perfect" (NRSV). How can Christ expect this of us?

Then I read Ephesians 2:8-9. Paul writes, "You are saved by God's grace because of your faith. This salvation is God's gift. It's not something you possessed." And yet, we read in James 2:17 that "faith by itself, if it has no works, is dead" (NRSV). What are we to do with these contradictions?

Wesleyan disciples know that Jesus, Paul, and James were trying to get across the same message. A key to this understanding is to realize that Matthew 5:48 has a double meaning. When Jesus said to "be perfect," his words could be translated as a prediction of the future: "you will be perfect." John Wesley believed that every commandment in Scripture is a hidden promise: What God expects us to do and be, he enables us to do and be by his grace. God's grace is constantly working in us to help transform our minds and lives.

Church as Recovery Group and Change Agent

What is the church's role in this? The church is not made up of fully sanctified persons who have achieved spiritual maturity and can call themselves perfect. Rather, the church is a body of people who have committed to journeying toward that holiness. Each Christian is a sinner who needs God's grace. By the grace of God, we are making progress as individuals and groups toward the goal of holiness.

Some people have described church as a recovery group, made up of people who have named their problems and are helping each other toward the goal of a sanctified life. Part of that help comes in teaching what God expects, so we are all clear on the goal. Part of that help comes in encouragement from those farther along the path, saying to beginners, "You can do it!" Part of that help comes because Christ has promised to be present through the means of grace, which the church provides.

As the body of Christ, we were told by Jesus, "You are the salt of the earth" and "You are the light of the world" (Matthew 5:13-14). Not only are we helping each other on our individual journeys, but we are also called to let God use us as a group to accomplish his larger purposes for the whole of creation. Where there is injustice, where there is hunger, where there is oppression or racism, the church is called to bear witness to God's amazing and universal love and to God's demands for justice, peace, and reconciliation through his creation.

"A Charge to Keep I Have"

Charles Wesley wrote a powerful hymn about our responsibility to participate in God's saving activity in the world:

TRADITIONAL

A charge to keep I have,
a God to glorify,
a never-dying soul to save,
and fit it for the sky.

To serve the present age,
my calling to fulfill;
O may it all my powers engage
to do my Master's will!

Arm me with jealous care,
as in thy sight to live,
and oh, thy servant, Lord,
prepare a strict account to give!

Help me to watch and pray,
and on thyself rely,
assured, if I my trust betray,
I shall forever die.[28]

CONTEMPORARY REPHRASING

I have one purpose to fulfill:
to bring glory to the God I love.
My never-dying soul is saved for eternity
and is being prepared even now for heaven.

My calling here on earth
is to serve with all I am—
my talents, my skills, my mind, my heart, my passion—
give it all to the will of God.

Help me, Lord, to take great care,
as I live my life for your pleasure.
I want to serve you, Lord.
May I leave a legacy of faithfulness to you.

Teach me, Lord, to look only to you,
to pray, to rely on you.
I know and am sure
that without you I would die.

7.

Invite Others on the Journey

God has blessed you so that you might be a blessing to others. Becoming a Christian means you have been saved for a purpose. That simple idea is a profound summary of the difference that the love of God makes in our lives.

The Wesleyan Way of salvation teaches that God in his amazing grace forgives our sins, reconciles our broken relationships with God, and heals us. Participating in the means of grace—regular worship, membership in the community, sharing of our needs through prayer and small group ministries, partaking in the sacraments of Holy Communion and baptism—opens us to the saving power of God and helps us on the journey.

The Christian life is not always easy. Each journey has its own challenges, problems, and opportunities. But it is a blessed life.

Yet, focusing on God's grace in our own lives can lead to a self-centered approach in which the question becomes "What's in it for me?" At our worst, Christians appear to be self-absorbed and inwardly focused.

The disciples had the same problem. They had seen Christ's miracles and had come to believe he was the Son of God. But when Jesus told them the Messiah would suffer, be rejected, and be killed, the disciples objected. This was not the powerful, successful, and kingly role they had been expecting:

> But Peter took hold of Jesus and scolding him, began to correct him. Jesus turned and looked at his disciples, then sternly corrected Peter: "Get behind me, Satan. You are not thinking God's thoughts but human thoughts." After calling the crowd together with his disciples, Jesus said to them, "All who want to come after me must say no to themselves, take up their cross, and follow me.

The Christian life is not always easy. But it is a blessed life.

All who want to save their lives will lose them. But all who lose their lives be-cause of me and because of the good news will save them. Why would people gain the whole world but lose their lives? What will people give in exchange for their lives? Whoever is ashamed of me and my words in this unfaithful and sinful generation, the Human One will be ashamed of that person when he comes in the Father's glory with the holy angels." (Mark 8:32-38)

Jesus was expressing the paradox of giving: If you want to save your life, you must lose it for God. If you want to find ultimate happiness, you must give it to God. Those who want to gain things for their own benefit will lose what they have and what they seek.

Christian blessings from God have a purpose: to offer blessings for others. This theme runs throughout the Bible, starting with the call of Abraham in Genesis. God says to Abram:

"Leave your land, your family, and your father's household for the land that I will show you. I will make of you a great nation and will bless you. I will make your name respected, and you will be a blessing. I will bless those who bless you, those who curse you I will curse; all the families of earth will be blessed because of you." (Genesis 12:1-3)

Again and again in the Old Testament, God requires Israel to take care of the widows, orphans, and aliens in their midst. The New Testament continues this message and focuses even more strongly on a life of sacrificial love.

Witnessing in Deed

No matter how much we do as Christians—even if we add up all the Christians in the world and what they do for God—it's not the whole story We believe that God is the one at work in the world, through grace, to save the creation and make it what God originally intended.

Thus, giving away your life for God is often described as being a witness to God's amazing grace. The risen Christ spoke to the disciples right before his ascension: "You will receive power when the Holy Spirit has come upon you; and you will be my wit-nesses in Jerusalem, in all Judea and Samaria, and to the end of the earth" (Acts 1:8).

Chapter 11 in the Book of Hebrews recounts the deeds of many people in the Old Testament, who by human measure did amazing things. But the author of Hebrews gives God the credit for what was done, because all those deeds were accomplished by faith. In two of the most powerful verses in Scripture, the author calls these persons "witnesses" saying:

So then let's also run the race that is laid out in front of us, since we have such a great cloud of witnesses surrounding us. Let's throw off any extra baggage, get rid of the sin that trips us up, and fix our eyes on Jesus, faith's pioneer and perfecter. He endured the cross, ignoring the shame, for the sake of the joy that was laid out in front of him, and sat down at the right side of God's throne. (Hebrews 12:1-2)

An Anchor for the Soul

How do you invite people on the journey? I think about the disciples. Andrew found his brother and invited him. Philip found Nathanael and repeated the words of Jesus: "Come and see; come and see" (John 1:39, 46). We don't have to go up to total strangers and ask them about their faith. We can go to people we know. I think about some of my closest friends in life. If they knew I had found something good—a new restaurant, a great investment—and I kept it to myself, they would probably let me have it. Well, faith should be the same.

I think sometimes we jump to things too early and think we have all the answers. We tell people what's right, what's wrong, and start preaching at them. That feels artificial, and I think God uses live bait, not artificial bait. When we don't know the answers, when things bother us, then God speaks through us using the authenticity of who we are. When I talk to people, they give me every reason why they can't stay in church, and sometimes I say, "You know, I think I agree. We're real people with doubts. We have our struggles. But we've found something that's like an anchor for the soul." Folks are looking for that.

If we follow the example of Jesus, we show grace and compassion and openness to other people's thinking. We understand that it's not arguments that change people's minds or hearts; it's the spirit of an individual. But we're not the ones doing it. We're just sowing seeds, and God is the one who does the watering and the growing and the producing of fruit. I'm not called to save anybody. The world already has a savior.

Rob Fuquay
Senior Pastor
St. Luke's United Methodist Church
Indianapolis, Indiana

From *The Wesleyan Way* DVD

Somehow, by grace through faith, our deeds of obedience to Christ are partly human action and partly divine action. When a Christian feeds the hungry in Christ's name, when a Christian heals the sick in Christ's name, when a Christian frees the oppressed in Christ's name or helps the poor in Christ's name, the deed is both a contribution to God's purposes and a witness pointing to God's love.

Sometimes skeptics rightly ask whether we as disciples of Jesus "walk the walk" or just "talk the talk." Even Jesus was aware of this problem, as seen in his parable of the man with two sons. In the parable, Jesus was addressing the chief priests and elders of the people when he said:

> "What do you think? A man had two sons. Now he came to the first and said, 'Son, go and work in the vineyard today.' 'No, I don't want to,' he replied. But later he changed his mind and went. The father said the same thing to the other son, who replied, 'Yes, sir.' But he didn't go. Which one of these two did his father's will? They said, "The first one." Jesus said to them, "I assure you that tax collectors and prostitutes are entering God's kingdom ahead of you." (Matthew 21:28-31)

John Wesley's sermon "The General Spread of the Gospel" makes the point that the biggest obstacle to the spread of Christianity is the behavior of Christians.[29] Wesley often talked about the amazing things God had done through the Methodist movement, but in his later years he complained that the movement had fallen away from the behaviors that first characterized it. Today, many of us who claim to be Wesleyan Christians do not adequately witness with our deeds.

In 1743, Wesley stated three "General Rules" to clarify the beliefs of the Methodist movement. Rueben P. Job, in his book *Three Simple Rules* (Nashville: Abingdon Press, 2009), has summarized the General Rules with modern language:

- Do no harm.
- Do good.
- Stay in love with God.

Wesley was very specific about the meaning of the first rule, "doing no harm," which is "avoiding evil of every kind, especially that which is most generally practiced."[30] Whether in the eighteenth century or the twenty-first, if Christians are committing evil acts, we are not bearing witness to Christ with our deeds

Wesley explained the second rule, "doing good," in this way: "being in every kind merciful after their power; as they have opportunity, doing good of every possible sort, and, as far as possible, to all men."[31] The rule then mentions doing good to people not only in their bodies but also in their souls.

The third rule, when fully explained in the Wesleyan Way, involves using the means of grace. We "stay in love with God" by allowing God's grace to shape our hearts, minds, and behaviors through the spiritual practices of worship, prayer, Bible study, and other ways of connecting with God.

Witnessing in Word

Though witnessing to the love of God with our deeds is essential to the Wesleyan Way of salvation, witnessing with our words is no less essential.

Consider a man whose arm is moving back and forth with a closed fist. How many different descriptions of his action can we give? He is

- swinging his arm
- exercising
- suffering from a nervous twitch in his muscles
- preparing to strike someone near him

All these are possible explanations for the man's actions. Then the man opens his fist and sends a small stone flying forward to splash in a nearby pond. The man smiles and says, "I was just throwing a rock."

In a similar way, the behaviors exhibited by Christians need explanation. People who look at our food pantries may not know that we are giving out food in the name of Christ. People who watch us worship may not understand why we sing and pray and preach. People who observe us lobby Congress for the well-being of the poor or for justice to immigrants may not see the deeper reasons of faith behind what we do.

Wesleyans believe it is God who does the saving work, and we are simply God's instruments, small parts of a larger process. We owe it to God and to those we serve to proclaim and explain that process and to give God the credit. You might call it "truth in labeling." If we help to change the world in Christ's name, then Christ should be credited.

Inviting Others

The other reason for witnessing verbally is described as part of the second General Rule: doing good to people in their souls. Many times Christians treat others as if they were soulless bodies. We feed them, offer them shelter, give them clothing, or heal their illnesses. What some people need is a saving relationship with Christ.

God has commanded us to love others, so if we become aware that one of our neighbors does not know Christ as Lord and Savior, we should figure out how to love that person well. Loving our neighbors means doing good to their souls as well as to their bodies.

A powerful slogan expressing that belief is: "Make a friend. Be a friend. Bring a friend to Christ." If a Christian really cares about someone and knows that the person's life would be happier and better as a disciple, then offering a relationship with Christ is the most logical and natural thing in the world.

Consider George and Jane. They are fine people who have good jobs and no obvious problems. They are married and have two preschool children. They share a group of friends with whom they do things on occasion. Both of them went to church sporadically as children, but during their college years they quit attending. George and Jane seem to have a life together that works for them. Do they need Christ? Should they belong to a church?

If the church is simply another club we belong to, then the answer may be no. After all, there are lots of different organizations that have merit.

If we believe that religion is a private matter and that it's impolite or unwise to discuss it with friends and acquaintances, then the answer may also be no. Conversations about religion can sometimes become heated and cause conflict, so why bring up the subject?

But if we believe that everyone needs Christ, then our course of action is clear. We should invite George and Jane to church, so they can know Christ and profess their faith in him.

Inviting People to Christ's Church

Wesleyan Christians believe that George and Jane need Christ, because Christ wants to be everyone's Lord and Savior. This way of salvation is the path to happiness, fulfillment, and eternal life.

Wesleyan Christians also believe that accepting Christ as Lord and Savior involves obedience to his commands. In the New Testament, there is no such thing as solitary Christianity. Belonging to Christ means belonging to his body, which is the church. The church offers the means of grace, which nourish Christian life and growth.

If George and Jane need Christ and the church, how will they make the connection? Though there are many paths they might take, the most significant and effective path is through conversation with Christians.

Every Christian should be an evangelist. This doesn't mean that all of us need to preach at a rally for Christ or appear on television asking for commitments. Evangelism can be as simple as asking a friend, "Do you have a church?" If the answer is yes, it's wonderful news and there's a new bond between the two of you. If the answer is no, or "I'm looking for a church to attend," then you can invite them to yours.

Such an invitation should never be given to someone who is active in a different church. That would be like stealing sheep from another part of the same flock. Wesleyans believe that Baptists, Roman Catholics, Episcopalians, Bible church members, Presbyterians, and other kinds of Christians are all disciples of Jesus. When someone transfers from one part of the flock to another, there's no net gain for the kingdom of God.

Invitations to church should be made lovingly and respectfully. Evangelism literally means "good message." The content of the message, in its simplest form, is that God loves you and wants a relationship to help you find fulfillment in life. To many people, that's good news. But in two thousand years, Christians have managed to deliver the invitation in a number of ways that come across as bad news. Christians have sometimes talked about sin, damnation, and hell as the initial expression of God's love. Christians have sometimes acted with hate, racism, sexism, exclusion, and greed so that our actions contradict the goodness of the words. We have even baptized people as we put them into slavery.

God is nudging those who are spiritually asleep to wake up and find the Lord.

Wesleyans believe that God's prevenient grace is already at work in the life of every person. God is nudging those who are spiritually asleep to wake up and find the Lord. Thus, an invitation is a way of recognizing what God is already doing in the person's life and adding our human voice to the Holy Spirit's urgings. The invitation might be to attend worship on Sunday morning, a Sunday school class party, or a Bible study. Many people want to make a difference for the needy, and for them the invitation might be to work on a mission project.

What if George and Jane were invited to help build a home for a poor family in the community? After a day of hard work for a worthy cause, they might learn that Christians can be a good group and that the church is a way of transforming the world. Next, they might be invited to a social event in someone's home. After that, an invitation to worship might lead them to know Christ.

Every Christian knows someone who needs an invitation. Every Christian is capable of making that invitation. At this most basic level, every Christian can be an evangelist.

Telling Your Story

Another way you can witness for Christ is to tell the story of your spiritual journey. 1 Peter 3:15-16 says, "Whenever anyone asks you to speak of your hope, be ready to defend it. Yet do this with respectful humility, maintaining a good conscience."

Sometimes you'll be asked, "Why are you a Christian?" Christ needs disciples who are willing and able to tell the story of how they came to faith.

There are as many different stories as there are Christians. I've told you parts of mine, including my upbringing as the son of a Methodist pastor and church musician, my summer mission experience, my drift away from the church, and my ride and conversation with the truck driver. My story has a couple of things in common with the stories of people outside or on the periphery of church. First, I have not always been a practicing Christian. I left the means of grace for a while. When I came back, I was searching, and it took a while to find the answer. Second, I did not have the powerful, instantaneous conversion experience that some others have had. My return to Christ was much more gradual.

Your story inevitably is different from mine, which simply illustrates the variety of ways that human beings encounter God. Any road leading to genuine discipleship is valid. Sharing our stories can help others along the way.

Mentoring Others

There is still another way of inviting others on the journey. Those who are considering becoming Christians often need a mentor or spiritual friend to walk with them. Christ needs people who can be that friend.

For some people considering the Christian journey, the issues and questions may be fairly basic and easy to discuss. Who is Christ? What is involved in baptism? How do you worship in church?

Other people have more difficult issues. They may have heard versions of Christianity that bother them. They may need help sorting out conflicting interpretations of Scripture. They may have had negative experiences with people who called themselves Christians. They may want to know if the Wesleyan Way of salvation is the same salvation they rejected at an earlier time in their lives. They may have deep questions about God and the power of evil in the world.

Mentors do not have all the answers. They do need the spiritual strength to share their perspective on the Christian faith when challenged. Mentors can point a seeker to resources and people who can help them work on their questions. They can guide seekers on the journey toward salvation.

Outwardly Focused Congregations

Healthy and growing congregations are focused outwardly. Their members are always looking for ways to bear witness for Christ through word and deed. They organize their small group activities to include service and witness. They work at radical hospitality. They seek ways to initiate spiritual conversations with those who don't have a church home. They are always ready to invite people outside the church to meet Christ.

Outwardly focused congregations have many ways in which outreach takes place. Some members who are not comfortable with verbal witness can help organize the communication, hospitality, and response systems of the church. Some members can make sure that signage and accessibility issues are addressed. Some can create and maintain the church's website, making sure it communicates clearly with unchurched persons in the community and beyond. Some can keep track of names and contact information, enabling others to build relationships effectively. All church members, in one way or another, will be focused on loving people in Jesus' name and reaching out to help them know the transforming love of God.

"Come Sinners, to the Gospel Feast"

Early Wesleyans were convinced that everyone needs Christ. They believed all were invited to know Jesus and be part of his body, the church. One of Charles Wesley's most famous hymns uses the idea of a heavenly banquet as the metaphor for invitation:

TRADITIONAL

Come, sinners, to the gospel feast;
let every soul be Jesus' guest.
Ye need not one be left behind,
for God hath bid all humankind.

Sent by my Lord, on you I call;
the invitation is to all.
Come, all the world! Come, sinner, thou!
All things in Christ are ready now.

Come, all ye souls by sin oppressed,
ye restless wanderers after rest;
ye poor, and maimed, and halt, and blind,
in Christ a hearty welcome find.

My message as from God receive;
ye all may come to Christ and live.
O let his love your hearts constrain,
nor suffer him to die in vain.

This is the time, no more delay!
This is the Lord's accepted day.
Come thou, this moment, at his call,
and live for him who died for all.[32]

CONTEMPORARY REPHRASING

Jesus has prepared a feast where all are welcome,
all sinners--everyone! We are guests at his table.
Leave no one behind. Come one, come all
and experience the gospel of Jesus Christ.

The Lord has sent me to invite you, to invite everyone.
All over the world, hear this invitation:
every need is met in Christ
and his love is ready for the taking even now.

Are you oppressed by sin?
Wandering aimlessly, seeking rest?
Poor? Abused? Scarred? Disabled?
You will find a welcome home in Christ!

God gave me the message:
come to Christ and find your life!
Give him your heart and live.
Don't let his death for you be in vain.

Don't wait any longer!
This is your time. The Lord is calling you today.
This very moment, come to him, hear his call,
and live for the one who died for you, who died for all.

8.

Christic No Matter What

Bad things still happen to good people. Following Christ does not mean protection from disaster, disappointment, or disease, in spite of what many people would like to believe.

We do believe that, taken as a whole, people with active faith commitments and high moral values do lead happier and more fulfilled lives. Comparing one person's path with another's path is always difficult and subjective, but Wesleyans teach and preach that any individual will be better off in this world and the world to come by journeying on the way of salvation.

Yet, there are many cases that cause people to ask, "Why did God allow this to happen?"

Sometimes the situations we face are not life-threatening. When a spouse is unfaithful and a marriage dissolves, we struggle with feelings of rejection, low self-esteem, and despair. When a job is lost because of an economic downturn, we wonder what to do and where to turn.

Sometimes, though, the situations involve life and death. One young mother of three boys was pregnant with her fourth when she was diagnosed with aggressive breast cancer. She was a leader in the children's choir and the midweek school program. She was an eager participant in Bible study groups. Her faith was strong, and she shared it freely with others. She was kind, loving, and generous. After a three-year fight, receiving the best medical care in the world, she died. Others have suffered natural disasters such as hurricanes, tsunamis, earthquakes, and tornadoes.

Why?

"Why did God allow this to happen?"

God Journeys with Us

The best answer to the persistent question *Why?* is that the Christian is never alone in dealing with them. Three truths may help explain the Christian point of view.

The first truth is that bad things happen in the world, and sometimes they affect good people. Why God allows this is a mystery. One man in my congregation was in his late nineties. He had been growing weaker for years and was ready to go to heaven. Then he fell and broke a hip. After one surgery he experienced great pain in learning to walk again, only to find that the other hip was also broken. He asked me, "Why doesn't God take me home now? Why is he letting me live so long?" I said, "Maybe you should ask the Lord that question when you get to heaven." The man smiled and said, "By then it won't matter."

We human beings are impatient and want to learn more of what God knows. In the story of Job, he asked God the question *Why?* and at a crucial point in the story, God replied:

> "Who is this darkening counsel with words lacking knowledge? Prepare yourself like a man; I will interrogate you, and you will respond to me. Where were you when I laid earth's foundations? Tell me if you know. Who set its measurements? Surely you know. Who stretched a measuring tape on it? On what were its footings sunk; who laid its cornerstone, while the morning stars sang in unison and all the divine beings shouted?" (Job 38:2-7)

God was basically saying, "Who are you to question my ways?" As much as we long to know why, there are some things we will never know in this life, and when we get to heaven, as the man in my congregation said, it truly won't matter.

The second truth, shown clearly in Scripture, is that God goes through tough times with us. God is love, and his steadfast love endures forever.[33] Through the record of God's dealing with Israel in the Old Testament, Scripture shows that God does not abandon his people regardless of what happens to them. A key summary of this teaching comes in Psalm 23:

> The LORD is my shepherd, I shall not want.
> He makes me lie down in green pastures; he leads me beside still waters;
> he restores my soul. He leads me in right paths for his name's sake.
> Even though I walk through the darkest valley, I fear no evil;
> for you are with me; your rod and your staff— they comfort me.
> You prepare a table before me in the presence of my enemies;
> you anoint my head with oil; my cup overflows.

Surely goodness and mercy shall follow me all the days of my life,
and I shall dwell in the house of the LORD my whole life long. (NRSV)

The image of God preparing a table for us to dine in the presence of our enemies is a powerful metaphor for how God can bless us in the midst of our troubles. Many times I have heard people in the midst of great difficulties—even in the process of dying—talk about how Christ was comforting them and how their faith was getting them through the hard times.

Sharing the Gospel

God has created a world of free agents.

There's a lot of stuff that goes on that God is not directly causing or planning or controlling. God has given free agents the possibility to do things, and the highest level of free agency is human beings. At the same time, God is always at work inside each of us, offering us grace and power to be what God wants us to be.

In our culture, there's a lot of religious junk out there. People have questions, and they go to funny places to find the answers. When I hear people talking about it, I often say to myself, Haven't they read John Wesley? Haven't they've heard of the Wesleyan Way?

I'm doing this study to connect with average folks, with seekers, with people who are asking important questions and want to know about living their lives as Jesus' disciples. Seven presenters are doing it with me—reaching out to people, helping them know Jesus, learning to live faithfully as Christian disciples. That's what gets me going.

I love sharing the gospel. I love explaining things in a way that makes sense. I love seeing the balance and occupying the extreme center. I'm convinced that that's what American culture needs today. It's why I've written this book.

Scott J. Jones
Bishop, The United Methodist Church
Kansas and Nebraska

From *The Wesleyan Way* DVD

The third truth was shown when the disciples asked Jesus whose sin had caused a particular man to be born blind. Jesus answered:

> "Neither he nor his parents. This happened so that God's mighty works might be displayed in him. While it's daytime, we must do the works of him who sent me. Night is coming when no one can work. While I am in the world, I am the light of the world." (John 9:3-5)

Jesus was telling us that, rather than dwell on why bad things have happened, we should view situations like this as opportunities to do God's work and make the world a better place.

Responding with Faith to Hard Times

The Wesleyan Way teaches that God's grace never leaves us. Even in the midst of difficulties, whether minor or severe, God is providing us with resources to overcome the problems. On the night before Christ died, he addressed this issue with the disciples:

> *The Wesleyan Way teaches that God's grace never leaves us.*

> I will ask the Father, and he will send another Companion, who will be with you forever. This Companion is the Spirit of Truth, whom the world can't receive because it neither sees him nor recognizes him. You know him, because he lives with you and will be with you. I won't leave you as orphans. I will come to you." (John 14:16-18)

When people who are suffering can experience the love and grace of God, they can see a way forward to overcome the hard times. The crucial element in such a situation is how people respond. They can reject God's grace and allow the suffering to overwhelm them, or they can respond with faith and allow God's grace maximum space to work.

My father's first heart attack, at age fifty-three, was fatal. My mother was forty-nine at the time. She was devastated. In the midst of her grief, though, she responded with faith. Two weeks after Dad's funeral, she told me we were going to drive three hours from our home in Durham, North Carolina, to see a doctor. I said we already had a doctor in Durham. She replied that this was a different kind of doctor. Then we drove to Waynesville, North Carolina, and met with Dr. Henry Perry. The following year, my fifty-year-old widowed mother spent the summer in the mountains of Bolivia, helping to run the Andean Rural Health Project, founded by Dr. Perry in 1979. She had wanted as a young girl to become a missionary but had married my father instead. She had loved being married to him and serving as a campus minister and musician, but now God was calling her into mission work. She spent much of the next twenty-five years leading mission teams to Bolivia and many other countries. God's grace gave her a new focus in life, and her faithful response allowed her to find the way to a new chapter in service to God.

Similar stories have been told many times about responses to disasters, disappointments, and deaths. Paul put it clearly in Romans 8:28: "We know that all things work together for good for those who love God, who are called according to his purpose" (NRSV). This powerful claim is one on which we can rely in the midst of difficult times. God does not cause the difficulties, but God is at work in every difficult situation for the good of his creation.

Death

Dying is a reality that all human beings face. Sometimes it strikes first in the death of our parents, friends, or loved ones. Sometimes it strikes our children. Sometimes it strikes in the form of a disaster or act of terrorism, and hundreds die at once.

Christians believe that life is good and that God intends for living beings to thrive and be protected. We go to great lengths to heal diseases and keep people living long lives. For many decades now, Wesleyan Christians have opposed the death penalty in order to minimize the taking of life.

But what happens after death?

Two key scriptural texts have shaped Christian thinking about life after death. First, Jesus engaged in a conversation with the two criminals who were crucified with him. One cursed Jesus, and the other defended him, maintaining that Jesus was innocent and saying, "Remember me when you come into your kingdom." Jesus replied, "I assure you that today you will be with me in paradise" (Luke 23:43).

A few years later Paul wrote to the church at Corinth:

Listen, I'm telling you a secret: all of us won't die, but we will all be changed—in an instant, in the blink of an eye, at the final trumpet. The trumpet will blast, and the dead will be raised with bodies that won't decay, and we will be changed. (1 Corinthians 15:51-57)

Heaven and Hell

Wesleyan Christians believe there is life after death and our relationship with Christ experienced on earth strongly shapes and perhaps determines what that relationship will be after we die. Those who know Christ as Lord and Savior while alive in earth expect to continue in relationship with Christ in life after death. John 3:16 says it clearly: "God so loved the world that he gave his only Son, so that everyone who believes in him won't perish but will have eternal life." The words "eternal life" are used many times in the New Testament to describe the promise that death is not the end of the story for those who love the Lord.

The Bible actually says very little about heaven and hell. Heaven is referred to in terms of eternal life and the alternative in terms of punishment where there is weeping and grinding of teeth (Matthew 13:42). Many Christians are troubled by the prospect of anyone going to hell. They ask how a loving God can send someone into eternal punishment. They point to Paul's claim in Romans 8:38-39:

> I'm convinced that nothing can separate us from God's love in Christ Jesus
> our Lord: not death or life, not angels or rulers, not present things or future
> things, not powers or height or depth, or any other thing that is created.

Wesleyans understand that everyone has received sufficient grace from God to be saved. The question, then, is whether we choose to use the grace God has provided. John Wesley said, "No man sins because he has not grace, but because he does not use the grace which he hath."[34]

Within the list of God's attributes, we count on God to know everything, to love everyone, to be righteous, and to be faithful for all time. Wesleyans believe that God loves us and allows us the free will to reject his love. Thus, whatever happens to us in eternity is a result of how we have responded to God's grace in this life.

We cannot know any particular person's state of salvation. God alone knows the heart of that person and will always judge fairly and correctly.

Christianity and Other Religions

Wesleyans affirm that God is righteous and just and will not condemn us to hell without giving us a realistic opportunity for salvation. When John Wesley began his ministry, there was a lot of discussion about how and whether people in Africa and America, who may never have heard the gospel preached, would be judged. Wesley had an interesting and thought-provoking response. He said that these people would be held accountable by God for the ways in which they responded to the grace they had been given preveniently.

After Jesus, the first generation of Christians spread the gospel in a multireligious and multicultural world. There were many options for belief and religious affiliation. And yet, the disciples knew that God had done something unique in the life, death,

CHRIST NO MATTER WHAT

and resurrection of Jesus. When Peter and John were arrested, they told the people, "Salvation can be found in no one else. Throughout the whole world, no other name has been given among humans through which we must be saved" (Acts 4:12). The goal of Christian evangelism is that someday everyone will have heard the truth about God, "So that at the name of Jesus everyone in heaven, on earth, and under the earth might bow and every tongue confess that Jesus Christ is Lord, to the glory of God the Father" (Philippians 2:10-11).

At the same time, following John Wesley's train of thought, we recognize that God has already been at work giving his grace preveniently to people who may not know what God did first through the Jews and then in Christ Jesus. We see that human beings have sought to worship God according to their best insights and that other religions offer valid perspectives. Though these religions are not the one true faith, they do present aspects of the truth. When Paul had the opportunity to preach at the Areopagus in Athens, he appealed to a religious practice already present among them. He said:

> "People of Athens, I see that you are very religious in every way. As I was walking through town and carefully observing your objects of worship, I even found an altar with this inscription: 'To an unknown God.' What you worship as unknown, I now proclaim to you." (Acts 17:22-23)

In the same way, Christian missionaries and evangelists look for points of connection with people of other faiths, suggesting ways in which the truth about God might partially be present in their beliefs and practices. Sometimes practices are carried over into Christianity as a way of making those connections. Famously, the celebration of Christ's birth was set for December 25 in order to build a connection with midwinter festivals that were popular in Rome. (It's a good guess that Jesus was born in the summertime, when shepherds would have been watching their flocks in the field at night.) Connecting with another religious practice and turning it into a Christian celebration was an evangelistic strategy that made sense at the time. It still does today.

Thus, while Wesleyans affirm that Christ is the only way to the Father, we also affirm that Christ may be at work through other religions in ways we don't know about and cannot understand this side of heaven. This is especially true when we take into account the evil things done by professing Christians over the centuries and the effect on other people. Also, God, in his omniscient judgment, may look at a Muslim or Jew or Buddhist and accept them into heaven because of the lack of a genuine opportunity to know Christ. At the same time, we do offer Christ to those in other religions, because Christ is the way, the truth, and the life.

End-Times

Though the end of an individual's life will certainly come someday, the end of the world is a topic that occasionally gets discussion among Christians. Both the Nicene and Apostles' creeds make reference to the second coming of Christ to judge the living and the dead. The books of Daniel and Revelation, along with a few verses in the Gospels, contain vivid imagery of end of the world and how those who believe in God will be treated during those times. Because wars and natural disasters are mentioned in these accounts, whenever such events occur, people begin to wonder again about the end of the world. Other major events such as the formation of modern Israel as a separate country, wars in the Middle East (the site of the biblical Armageddon), and the start of the second millennium A.D. have triggered associations with the end-times.

One of the most important scriptural texts about predicting the end of the world comes from Jesus. After describing some of the signs, he said in Matthew 24:36, "But nobody knows when that day or hour will come, not the heavenly angels and not the Son. Only the Father knows." Based on this text, not even Jesus while he was on earth knew when these things would happen.

Modern science has changed the way Wesleyans think about the beginning and end of the world and the time frames involved. Though some Christians see science and faith as being in conflict, Wesleyans see them as complementary, as described by one denomination:

> We recognize science as a legitimate interpretation of God's natural world. We affirm the validity of the claims of science in describing the natural world and in determining what is scientific. We preclude science from making authoritative claims about theological issues and theology from making authoritative claims about scientific issues. We find that science's descriptions of cosmological, geological, and biological evolution are not in conflict with theology.[35]

Most scientists believe that the world is billions of years old and that any claim of an end to the universe in the next thousand years is nonsensical. Wesleyans are open to understanding the second coming of Christ in light of this science, without attempting to predict a time frame that violates scientific truth.

Following Christ Is a Way of Life

Whatever happens in our lives, the fundamental principle that guides discipleship is to follow Christ in everything we think, say, and do. The triune God is the ultimate reality of the universe, and God has created each of us for a purpose—to love God and neighbor in everything.

We do so in community. Christ saves individuals, but salvation always involves being formed into the body of Christ, which is the church. The church has taken different forms at various points in history, but whatever form it has taken, participation in the gathered community of believers has never been optional.

There is no way of life better than following Jesus. It involves giving of ourselves, but also being blessed. It means becoming who we are meant to be and finding joy, meaning, and purpose in life. When bad things come our way, we find the strength and grace to thrive despite the difficulties. When we receive blessings, we find they were given for a larger purpose.

"Christ the Lord Is Risen Today"

One of Charles Wesley's most powerful hymns is normally sung on Easter, but for Christians every Sunday is Easter. Christ's resurrection was God's powerful promise of eternal life and a sign of how we are to live here on earth. The hymn's final stanza describes soaring where Christ has led. The Wesleyan Way of salvation is a way of living triumphantly, through the grace of God.

TRADITIONAL	CONTEMPORARY REPHRASING
Christ the Lord is risen today, Alleluia! Earth and heaven in chorus say, Alleluia! Raise your joys and triumphs high, Alleluia! Sing, ye heavens, and earth reply, Alleluia!	Christ the Lord is risen today, praise him! All of earth and heaven sing together, praise him! Lift up your praises as high as you can, praise him! The heavens sing first and the earth replies, praise him!
Love's redeeming work is done, Alleluia! Fought the fight, the battle won, Alleluia! Death in vain forbids him rise, Alleluia! Christ has opened paradise, Alleluia!	The God of Love has finished redeeming us, praise him! The battle for our hearts has been won by God, praise him! If he hadn't risen, his death would be in vain, but praise him! He rose again and opened up the heavens to us. Praise him!
Lives again our glorious King, Alleluia! Where, O death, is now thy sting? Alleluia! Once he died our souls to save, Alleluia! Where's thy victory, boasting grave? Alleluia!	He was dead, but Christ rose again, praise him! What power does death have over us now? None, praise him! He died, once for all, to save us, praise him! Death may have thought it had bragging rights, but, praise him, death has no victory over us.
Soar we now where Christ has led, Alleluia! Following our exalted Head, Alleluia! Made like him, like him we rise, Alleluia! Ours the cross, the grave, the skies, Alleluia!	Now, we soar with Jesus all the way to heaven, praise him! We follow him, our mighty leader, praise him! We are made like him and we will rise like he did, praise him! We get to claim his cross, his grave, and his victory over death as our own, praise him!
Hail the Lord of earth and heaven, Alleluia! Praise to thee by both be given, Alleluia! Thee we greet triumphant now, Alleluia! Hail the Resurrection, thou, Alleluia!	Praise the Lord of earth and heaven, praise him! Let all of earth and heaven praise God! Earth and heaven come before God to praise him. We praise God for the resurrection of Christ! Praise God!
King of glory, soul of bliss, Alleluia! Everlasting life is this, Alleluia! Thee to know, thy power to prove, Alleluia! Thus to sing, and thus to love, Alleluia!36	God is our King, our soul knows pure joy, praise him! This is everlasting life: to know God, to trust his power, to sing his praises, and to love him. Praise him!

Acknowledgments

The Wesleyan movement is blessed with a large number of talented scholars, pastors, and lay leaders. Seven of them have joined me in this project, and they have been supported by staff persons in their congregations. They are daily being used by God to help people along the Wesleyan Way.

The rediscovery of John Wesley and his importance for twentieth- and twenty-first-century people has had many participants. Albert Outler was a key leader in that effort. His teaching, writing, and personal encouragement opened new understandings for me. Richard Heitzenrater and John Deschner were my teachers who shared their methods and insights along my academic journey. Randy Maddox, Ted Campbell, Rebekah Miles, Rex Matthews, Stephen Gunter, Paul Chilcote, Laceye Warner, William Abraham, and Ken Collins have been fellow travelers along the way. I have benefited greatly from conversations, books, and joint research in understanding Wesley and the Wesleyan movement.

Many thanks to Jenny Youngman, who wrote the contemporary rephrasings of hymns at the end of the chapters.

Notes

Chapter 1

1. UMH, 359.

2. *Works of John Wesley*, 3:585.

3. BOD, ¶104, p. 71.

4. UMH, 57.

Chapter 2

5. See a summary at http://www.anselm.edu/homepage/dbanach/anselm.htm.

6. John Wesley, *Explanatory Notes Upon the New Testament*, 1 John 4:8.

7. UMH, 384.

8. UMH, 880.

9. UMH, 139.

10. Translated by D. M. Kay, http://www.earlychristianwritings.com/text/aristides-kay.html.

11. UMII, 88.

Chapter 3

12. *John Wesley Letters*, February 24, 1791.

13. *Works of John Wesley*, 3:207.

14. BOD, ¶125, pp. 93–94.

15. UMH, 355.

Chapter 4

16. UMH, 378.

17. Augustine, *The Confessions*, 1.1.

18. UMH, 339.

19. UMH, 363.

20. UMH, 363.

Chapter 5

21. UMH, 627.

22. *Works of John Wesley*, 1:105. The Latin phrase means "man of one book."

23. BOD, ¶104, p. 71.

24. *Disciple: Becoming Disciples Through Bible Study*, Week 1 video (Nashville, TN: Graded Press, 1987).

25. *Works of John Wesley*, 1:533.

26. UMH, 378.

Chapter 6

27. *Works of John Wesley*, 2:82.
28. UMH, 413.

Chapter 7

29. *Works of John Wesley*, 2:495.
30. BOD, ¶104, p. 76.
31. BOD, ¶104, p. 77.
32. UMH, 339.

Chapter 8

33. See Psalm 119 where that phrase is repeated many times.
34. *Works of John Wesley*, 3:207.
35. BOD, ¶160, p. 107.
36. UMH, 302.